MW01484361

FROM THE STREETS

TO THE THRONE

Isaiah Blancas

Copyright © 2019 by Isaiah Blancas

All rights reserved. No part of this publication my be reproduced, distributed, or transmitted in any form or by any means, including photocopying, recording, or other electronic or mechanical methods, without the prior written permission of the publisher, except in the case of brief quotations embodied in critical reviews and certain other noncommercial uses permitted by copyright law. For permission requests, write to the publisher at the address below.

Isaiah Blancas
P. O. Box 339
Fort Stockton, Tx 79735

IsaiahVRC@gmail.com


Cover Concept: Victor Lopez
Image El Paso: Hadley Paul Garland
Image Torn Paper: TeroVesalainen from Pixabay

Scriptures marked ESV are taken from The Holy Bible, English Standard Version. ESV® Permanent Text Edition® (2016). Copyright © 2001 by Crossway Bibles, a publishing ministry of Good News Publishers.

# Contents

Dedication

I dedicate this book to my grandmothers Rosemary Sandoval and Racheal Hornedo Blancas, my heroes.

Grandmother Rosemary, without your prayers and endless sacrifice and dedication to the call of God on your life, I would have been lost. You are a true example of God's unfailing love and grace. You were always in my ear testifying about your great God, which is now my great God. When everyone else in this life abandoned me, you were always there. Even when I was locked up in countless facilities and cells, you showed me love when even my own parents never cared to visit me. You were there showing me what I now know is God's love. I love you, Grandma, and thank God for your life. I will forever be grateful to you for everything you did for me in this lifetime.

Grandmother Racheal, thank you for the love and friendship. You showed me what a true friend is while you were alive on earth. I will see you one day in heaven. Thank you for dreaming big and inspiring me to do the same. Thank you for making me feel special when no one else did. I will forever love you and be thankful to God for the years He allowed me to spend with you on this earth. You were my best friend, someone I could talk to about anything.

You both will forever be my heroes that God placed on this earth just so I could see a glimpse a hope of what was to come when I accepted Jesus Christ as my Lord and Savior. You both have forever touched my heart and live in my heart. May I be as good an example to my kids and grandchildren as you were to me. Thank you again for your tender hearts towards your grandson's life. You both made a tremendous difference in me. I love you both with all my heart,

Your grandson, Isaiah Blancas

Forward

I had the honor of meeting Isaiah Blancas when he was a guest on my show. Even though our show is a secular show, Isaiah shared his testimony of how God changed his life. Our audience was deeply touched by his story. Even though it was brief it was still powerful. As I researched more on the gang that he came from, it became apparent to me that this was no ordinary street gang. We are talking about the darkest and the most evil of all gangs.

Isaiah's book gives insight into the gang world and how people can come to a point in their life where human life no longer matters. Most of all, this book will show you the power of God to change anyone and how he can use the weakest in God's kingdom to reach the strongest and most evil in this world.  Whether you are trying to reach someone involved in drugs or gangs, or if you feel that you have done so much evil that you cannot be forgiven, this book will change your mind.

**GILBERT ESQUIVEL**
**Comedian**
**Host of G's Nightowl Coffee Show**

## What People Are Saying

I met Isaiah back in 2000 he was about 21 years old  the Lord opened doors for me to go minister to the men at the Avalon Correctional Center in Horizon City, Texas  a little town bordering El Paso, Texas. I was told that you could not even look at Isaiah sideways because he would literally beat the pulp out of you if you looked at him. I understood that deep down in his soul Isaiah was hurting big time, and I realized that he truly did not know what the love of God was because of what he experienced from 9 years-old to 21 years-old. He had been truly rejected and not genuinely loved from his immediate family. I believe with all my heart and soul that this book will reveal to every person that reads it that it is never too late to change and that nothing is impossible for GOD. If He can change the heart of a young man that truly did not know what the  love of God can do for you he can do it for anybody that is willing to say I am sick and tired of being sick and tired. We truly need to understand that we are living in a fatherless nation. I declare that every man that reads this book will be prepared and empowered to impact lives in Jesus mighty name! The impact of this book will be astounding to all who read it; only God can do what He did for Isaiah. I truly believe there are many like Isaiah today, needing a Savior. If He can change Isaiah Blancas, He can change radically anybody that will open and read this book. All the honor and glory is given to our heavenly Father for what he did in the life of my precious godly son, Isaiah Blancas, in JESUS name.

*Chaplain Gina Montes*

Isaiah Blancas is a true man of God and a true warrior for the kingdom of God. I first heard Isaiah speak at a men's recovery group in San Fernando California in early 2018.  He delivered a powerful testimony and a message of hope and we bonded immediately. One thing I love is a good testimony. When people count you out, God doesn't.  1 Corinthians 1:27 But God chose the foolish things of the world to confound the wise. (KJV) There is no doubt that God has a special calling in Isaiah's life. Join him as he takes you through a riveting journey growing up in the streets of El Paso, Texas and Juarez, Mexico. A true story of how God took him from the streets to the throne. Only God can do the impossible. A must read.

*Brother Sal Rodriguez, Drummer for the rock band, WAR*

The miraculous of God is alive and well today. In this book, From the Streets to the Throne, the testimony of God's promise, forgiveness, and mercy is so clearly seen in Isaiah Blancas' life. You will see how God can take a kid from the streets of gangs to God, sculpturing a young man into a champion for God. Isaiah has allowed heaven to mold him, heal him, and transform his life as God the Potter and Isaiah the clay. Enjoy this book about the great story of God's power and his faithfulness.

***Pastor Joshua Krishna, Lead Pastor, Embassy***

Over the past year I've come to know my Brother Isaiah Blancas and his deep desire to further the Kingdom and Gospel of our Lord Jesus Christ. The life that God redeemed him from truly represents God's power, love, and compassion for those that are the worst of the worst. Isaiah's testimony demonstrates to the world that in Christ there is victory. Much respect and love to my Brother Isaiah. ***Sensei William "Blinky" Rodriguez, servant of Jesus Christ, Executive Director CIS (Communities in Schools)***

The gripping account of the life of Isaiah Blancas will pull you into a story of the reality of the streets. His call to action to choose a different life over the troubles that face many youth is a reality that many people do not comprehend. This compelling and triumphant memoir will make you believe that anyone with the most troubled life can overcome the ordeals of life to change the world for the better. Isaiah tells a story that is both deeply personal and completely universal - one that will resonate deeply with anyone that believes that the power of God can create a new human being and a new positive life. I highly recommend this powerful book that will surely change the lives of many.               ***Carlo Mendo, CEO//Munvio***

*I was once told your story will either be a prison you live in or a platform you stand on. From the Streets to the Throne is an incredible story of how Isaiah has taken his story and turned it into a platform. He's beautifully used his scars to tell his story. Few people would have predicted that a guy from El Paso, Texas would someday impact so many. This book reminds us that ANYTHING IS POSSIBLE! His life is such a great example of when you mix unadulterated focus on Jesus, ferocious faith and availability with the grace of God. Never have I met anyone as humble, passionate and sold out to the mandate of Heaven as Isaiah. He is special and so is this book. Do your soul a favor and check it out.*

**Pastor Victor Lopez, Gracepoint Church, Fort Stockton, Texas**

**From the Streets to the Throne**

**By Isaiah Blancas**

**With Jody Bailey Day**

1.

A Childhood Cut Short


My dad used to buy me things, all I had to do was ask. He took me places and spent time with me. Happiness ruled in our El Paso, Texas home. We moved to Brownsville in the late 1980s. I was just a happy seven-year-old playing in the grass and watching fireflies in the night sky. Dad took my mom, my little sister, and I to the ocean. I loved my boogie board and I knocked around with my friends. Once, I gashed my foot, and my parents lovingly bandaged the deep cut and comforted me. I liked school and made good grades.

We stayed in Brownsville a year, and then moved back to El Paso. We had family there that I loved spending time with, but my favorite thing was being with Mom and Dad. I knew nothing but love and security.

I didn't know that my childhood would soon be over.

Back in El Paso, Dad wasn't around very much. I noticed that he came home really late, and sometimes not at all. I missed him, but I didn't know anything was wrong. My parents' relationship began to deteriorate. I didn't understand.

Gang members lived in our apartment complex. I retreated from the unhappiness at home by hanging out with them. I started to smoke cigarettes, steal candy, toys and beer. Yes, I was eight.

My dad argued with my mom about her letting me hang with the gang. They were so much older than me. I dressed like them, which at the time reflected Mexican gangsters from the 1950s and 1960s era. We wore Dickies, white muscle shirts, and bombitas, which were black shiny steel toe shoes, or Nike Cortez. My parents fought about it.

Dad spent his time partying and doing drugs. He cheated on my mom with her sister-in-law. One night a loud knocking on the door woke me up. The police brought my dad home, beaten to a pulp. I discovered later that my mom's brothers did it. If the police hadn't intervened, they would have killed him. That was the plan, anyway.

Those uncles were in gangs, prison gangs, and some were in the Mafia. They had a green light on my dad, which is a death sentence. They were, and still are, real street guys who are much respected in the Texas prison gang system.

The trouble at home scared and confused me. I avoided it by focusing on my gang friends. They took a liking to me and I was infatuated with them. I wanted to be like them. They didn't care anything about the law. Little by little I started breaking the rules. I made my little sister steal cigarettes for me. I thought I was so cool.

An older cousin, that I admired, Izzy, got me into skateboarding with his friends. I loved it as something positive in the crumbling security around me. Dad came around less and less. We moved to a different apartment complex that was nowhere near as nice as our previous one. Everything about it resembled my eight-year-old life - fading.

When Dad did come around, he and Mom didn't get along.  They fought the last time I saw him. Mom had made spaghetti for dinner. They started cussing at one another. Dad threw spaghetti all over the walls. As the dishes crashed to the floor, he said, "I'm leaving. You'll never see me again!"

I wanted to go with him. I pulled on his jacket and begged. "Dad, I want to go with you."

"I can't take you with me, Son."

I loved him so much.

My mom held a grudge against me because I clung to my dad that night. It seemed like she loved my sister more than me after that. It made me mad at my sister and I burned her Barbie dolls. That caused Mom to bust up a radio that I cherished. Dad had given it to me. I told her that night, "I want to go live with Dad."

I missed my dad playing guitar. He could also play piano. He left behind a *Bad Company* tape. I listened to it to feel near him.

My mom had mental problems. I didn't know this until much later. Her condition escalated after Dad left. I knew he'd never come back. We moved again, and this time to a really bad neighborhood called the Jackie Robinson Projects. That's where I met the PVJ WSL (West Side Locos) gang. Just walking through the neighborhood where hard-core gang members hung out on every corner was dangerous to a nine-year-old. They were covered with tattoos, and you just knew they'd been in and out of jail or prison. These older guys drank barrels of beer and did drugs in the streets. Any kid walking down the block was in danger of a beating or worse. The gang members deliberately intimidated us. "Where you from?" they'd call, meaning "What gang are you from?" I was terrified and felt out of place. My early life of a loving family was already just a memory, and I knew things would never be the same again.

I had to embrace my new reality. I witnessed beatings, stabbings, and shootings. Kids in the neighborhood were in the gangs, and they became my friends. Most of them came from broken homes with an absent parent or both. If they did have parents, they were likely in the gangs too. Some of my friends' moms were prostitutes and/or drug dealers in the PVJ gang. Some of the fathers dealt drugs with the cartels or were in prison gangs. My friend Koko's dad was doing a life sentence in prison. Koko met him for the first time there.

Things at home with Mom became horrible. She said things like, "You look like your dad." She resented me. I believe she was at a breaking point in her life, and she took it out on me. Hopelessness crept into my heart.

Spray paint gang graffiti was everywhere. I witnessed terrible gang fights. The whole thing shocked my system to the point that I tried to hang out with kids not in the gang. I remember the sheer panic that would come upon us when the older guys from the Jackie's gang would come walking through the street. We would run up to where we hung out yelling, "The guys from Jackie's are coming! Run and hide!" Some would jump through windows into their apartments and some of the kids would hide behind apartments or wherever they could. Even as a kid I could tell who was running the show. These frightened children were delinquents themselves, and some already had house arrest bracelets around their ankles from being in the detention home, which is juvenile jail in El Paso. Some already had tattoos and some, if not all were in gangs themselves.

I began to realize that it was better to fit in than to be in constant terror. Still, even with all I'd seen, I was clueless about the lifestyle.

Around this time I met my friend Victor, nick-named Fish. We hung around together a lot. We started huffing spray paint, and even tried to start a little gang of our own. It's pretty funny now, looking back. Fish and I got our first tattoos together when I was nine, he was a little older, probably eleven. We were as close as brothers and tried to look out for each other.

I had other friends, and enemies, because of who I was trying to be. I tried to act like a hardcore little gang member, and you really couldn't trust too many growing up in that area. I argued with a so-called friend, and got beat up, a normal occurrence in that neighborhood. The beating was so bad I had to go the hospital. The doctor told my mom that if I got injured in my eye area again, I'd lose my vision.

It didn't take a rocket scientist to see the path where my life was headed.

2.

## A Hardened Heart

I started to pick on other kids and bully them. That's when I met others around my age that lived in the Jackie's projects. I met my friends Valdo, his older brother Manny, and Cruz. We called Valdo's mom "The Godmother." We all went to the same elementary school. Valdo and Manny were both from the Jackie's gang and Cruz's family lived in the Jackie's projects since the 1970's.

My reputation grew as a kid who didn't care. I made some enemies that were around my age from a gang that also had a bad reputation. Those kids would sometimes show up at my house and ask my mom if I was home. They waited for me with bats and knives to beat me up if I came outside. Most moms wouldn't think it unusual for kids that young to be asking for their son to come out. I think my mom thought they were just kids wanting to play with me.

Fish, Valdo, Cruz and I started hanging around in that neighborhood huffing spray paint, smoking marijuana, taking pills, or using heroin. This was an everyday occurrence. I know it sounds crazy, but it was normal for us. We had no parental guidance and so we looked up to the older guys we would see in the neighborhood. But they were gangsters, guys who sold and did drugs, guys who had money through illegal means. They had pretty girls around them, and in our eyes they were super stars. Most kids who lived in better areas probably would tell you they wanted to be doctors or lawyers when they grew up. We wanted to be gangsters. That was our atmosphere and what we aspired to be.

At first we would hang around my apartment which was just up the street from the Jackie's projects. Valdo would steal a little bit of weed from his brother. My mom used to paint the parking lines where cars parked in front of our apartments, and she always had around thirty to forty cans of spray paint in a closet in our apartment. I would steal two or three spray paint cans so we could huff them. We sprayed paint onto a sock, folded it and huffed it. Or we sprayed it into a soda can and put a rock in it. If the paint was getting hard, you would shake the rocks to loosen the paint so you could stay high longer.

Getting high helped us forget about our lives. At least that's how I felt. We huffed so much paint that all the cans in mom's closet were empty.  Mom asked me a few times, "Did you grab the spray paint cans?" and of course I denied everything. I'd say, "They must have sold you empty cans." She'd go get more and we'd do the same thing.

We started hanging around in the Jackie's projects because Manny was in that gang. We were allowed to hang around them. I'm not saying it wasn't dangerous because it was, but our lives were spiraling out of control even at that young age.  Gang graffiti on the walls mesmerized me - Klick Klick Bang Bang WS PVJ Gang - and nicknames such as Sincerely Spider, Yogi, Joker, Speedy, and many others. I hung out there until late at night. We would always see helicopters and cops going through the Jackie's projects as guys from the gang would be running through the projects, trying to get away from the law.  The older guys ran from the law because they were doing beer runs, robbing houses, or breaking into the elementary and middle school stealing computers for fast money.

We started ditching school and doing drugs. I was failing all my classes. I went to the detention home for the first time for stealing beer. I just did it to be bad, I didn't really drink it.  I didn't know it then, but my friends and I would be spending a lot of time in the detention home. My heart grew colder and colder, and fear gradually left my mindset.

I understood I had to be bold, fearless, and heartless to make a name for myself.

3.

## On the Streets

Things at home became unbearable for me and for my mom too. She kept telling me that I looked like my father. This is when my mom first kicked me out. She didn't allow me back in the house for three days. It hurt terribly, but I did not cry. I started taking out my emotions in a different way, now with anger and hate. I hated her, but I also hated my dad for leaving me for my aunt and fleeing to California. Mom was always kicking me out and I turned to the streets more and more.  My anger and hate grew.

One day my mom, my sister and I were driving on the east side of El Paso and for no reason my mom started yelling at me, again telling me how much I looked like my dad. She stopped the car and told me to get out. She drove off and it made me feel horrible. I had to walk twenty miles to get back home to west El Paso.  I was nine.

I didn't get home until one or two a.m. the next morning. I did have other family in El Paso, but there were no cell phones 1980s. There were pay phones, but I didn't have any phone numbers with me, and I didn't really know where they lived. My mom was so angry at everyone; she pushed every family member away. As a matter of fact, she has little to no contact with any family members to this very day.

Things at school were just as bad. The elementary school I attended kicked me out after many incidents. In those days they would spank your behind with a paddle. I was in trouble so much that I was always getting spanked by the principals. There were many school suspensions, so I guess they had enough of me and expelled me. It wouldn't be the last time for El Paso schools systems to kick me out.  I was a handful and had been kicked out of about eight schools that year. No one wanted to deal with me so I ended up in the BIC program (Behavior Intervention Center) at a school for the worst kids. Even there I was one of the worst. In one particular school there was actually a lock down cell, similar to a lock down cell at the juvenile detention home jail. I spent a lot of time in that room. There was nothing in there and when you were inside it, there was no door knob, just a little thick glass window in the middle of the metal door. They put troublemakers in that room for the whole day. I even had to eat in there. I felt it was getting me ready for the type of lifestyle I was going to live.

The school called my mom when I was in trouble, but she never came. She must have put my Grandma Rosemary down as a call reference because she started showing up and sometimes sitting with me in the classroom. She sat with me sometimes weeks at a time, sometimes even months. I don't think she expected her grandson to be such a delinquent. Grandma told me later in life that the first time she was called and she went into the office that the desk clerk was bubbly and seemed really happy saying "Ma'am, how can I help you?" Grandma answered, "I'm here for Isaiah Blancas." The lady's demeanor totally changed, saying, "Oh, that kid is going to prison." Grandma got mad and said, "That will never happen." Grandma Rosemary later said she felt like she'd have to eat her words.

I started hanging around the Jackie's projects a lot more, getting into trouble. My mom kicked me out a lot more often, sometimes weeks at a time, then months. To be honest, I can recall being home with my mom and little sister very little. By the time I was nine and a half, I was pretty much on my own until I was twelve. If it snowed I had to walk to an apartment complex, miles away that had a sauna by the pool area. I would go in there at night to sleep and keep warm. I had to start stealing shoes, food, and clothes to try to take care of myself. It was rough, and not just for me but for a lot of kids in the Jackie's area. We were pretty poor and would steal to have just basic things normal kids had in a normal home. We walked everywhere or we took a bus to get around. Sometimes we'd go to Peter Piper Pizza and wait for people to eat, and then we'd eat their leftover pizza. This really made me mad because it reminded me of when my relationship with my mom was pretty good. She used to buy pizza for me and my friends.

I started going in and out of the detention center more and more, and I wasn't alone. I would see my friends from Jackie's in there too. The first time I spent a week in the detention home I actually prayed to God. I thought about when I had my parents in my life and they would take me to church. To be honest, I didn't remember too much when I left church, but it was another precious memory of my past. They tried to teach us to pray at the detention center. They had Bibles. I can remember actually praying and saying, "God if you get me outta here I will change and never come back." I was mad at God and at life.

The Jackie's gang was known in the detention home for being tough. You could see PvJ WSL scraped into the metal doors throughout the facility. Older guys from the neighborhood had already done time there and started going to adult jails and prisons in the Texas Department of Corrections. So there I was. I had to be tough in there and hold my ground, especially coming from the Jackie's neighborhood. One of the kids in there would get beat up all the time and the other kids sexually assaulted him. The victim acted like he liked it. In my view, he was just trying to hide his hurt and pain. That was definitely not going to happen to me. Things got crazier and crazier when I was released back into the streets.

My little friends and I were little delinquents by the time I turned ten, always doing something wrong or bad, and the older guys from Jackie's started noticing us and wanted us to hang around them. Nothing good ever happened in my neighborhood and it seemed like every time my friends came out of their house and we met up, there were always older guys from Jackie's around, up to nothing good. It was very hard for me to stay or be positive. As soon as you walked out of your place, you would see guys doing drugs or huddling up together to see what kind of crimes we would be participating in. We would steal from houses, stores or the nearby mall. What kind of drugs would we be getting into that day? Where we would be drinking alcohol or what party would we go to?

The older guys planned parties in the middle of the desert. The guys from Jackie's had desert areas in back of the projects where they would party. There were old couches out there where we would get together, and the older guys would buy barrels of beer and get crazy up in that desert. I remember they always had pretty girls that would party with them. It was crazy to say the least. I saw a lot of my older homeboys sick and throwing up because they needed a fix of heroine. So they would steal whatever they needed to make that happen. The even stole hand soap. The got a dollar for every ten hand soaps they would steal. They would catch a bus to downtown and go to the Tiradero, which was in the Segundo Barrio, the 2nd ward in El Paso. This was a notorious neighborhood back in the 80s and 90s. As matter of fact, it was so bad back then that people who would go party in Juarez, Mexico, which everyone in the world considers one of the most dangerous places on earth until this very day, would be scared to walk across the border into the Segundo Barrio neighborhood.  In my time, if you were not known in that neighborhood, and you crossed the bridge from Mexico into the U.S., you would be beaten up badly by one of the worst prison gangs ever to exist. They controlled that area with an iron fist. If you were lucky, and I do mean lucky, because a lot of times it was worse, they would leave you in your underwear and steal everything from you, shoes and all.

This is where my older homeboys would often get their drugs or deal. Many times they would take us down there with them, either in a car or the bus. The Jackie's gang was known there, so we were allowed to enter. It was still dangerous, but a lot of the older homeboys were part of the prison gang that controlled all El Paso. We still got in fights with street gangs though, sometimes down in that area.

By the time I turned eleven, my friends and I were being trained by the older members of Jackie's to be hard core gang members. In those times other gangs would jump you into the gang once. "Jumped in" is when your other friends from your neighborhood gang would beat you up badly for maybe five minutes. Maybe three to seven guys would beat you up, and then you would be part of the gang.

I know it might sound stupid or ignorant, but if you grew up like I did, it makes perfect sense.

4.

## Jackie's Gang

The Jackie's gang was totally different. They always beat us up to see if we were down to be a part. Sometimes they would beat you up for months, sometimes years just to see if you had what it took to be a part of their gang. I was beaten up very badly by seven guys from Jackie's when I was twelve years old. I was going into Valdo and Manny's apartment in the Jackie's projects, all beat up bruised and full of blood. Manny came in and said, "Hey, Huero!" which was the knick-name they gave me which meant white boy in English, because of my light skin. He said, "Huero, come back outside cause they're gonna think you're weak."

I said, "What? They just beat the hell out of me. I'm hurt, I ain't weak." I went outside anyway. There must have been twenty-five to thirty-five of us out that night hanging around. I got beat up by the most feared ones, but I do remember going back out and standing my ground. At least that's what I thought in my head, and it didn't stop there. They beat me up multiple times for a few years until I was a full-fledged PVJ WSL gang member. I remember other kids my age getting beat up and then actually moving from the projects. The older guys would laugh and call them 'rucas' which means girls. One kid got beat up by my homeboy Koko. It was so bad that his teeth had been knocked out, and his gums torn open. He had to get stitches on his gums.

That's how it was for me at thirteen-years-old. Fish, Valdo, Cruz and I were the first ones to be part of the Jackie's gang at our age. Many others started getting in. We were already a pretty big gang but we started growing and getting even bigger. I was always on the streets because I was not wanted at home. The PvJ gang became my family. We were closer than blood brothers. I was big time into drugs and going in and out of the detention home jail. My friends were doing the exact same things the old school homeboys were doing before us – stealing, doing drugs, and spray painting walls. Our nick-names were all over the walls. You would see

PVJ WSL Huero, Fish, Walnut, and Crook, all over the place on the walls in our neighborhood and throughout El Paso.

A lot of my friends and I did months, then years behind bars for the lifestyle we had grown accustomed to. I was always in the streets or the detention home. It was a thrill to me, and I started to love the lifestyle I was living.

5.

## Family and School

At this point my two grandmas, who are my heroes, began to figure out something was wrong. My mom didn't keep in contact with them. My grandma from California, Rachael Blancas, actually found out where I was hanging around and would go to the Jackie's projects sometimes, even at night, to try to find me. This was not safe at all. A lot of my homeboys would rob anyone at any time, but from what I understand she would give them my name and since they knew me and I was part of the gang they would leave her alone. I stayed from house to house or in the desert. She looked for me for months until she finally found me. When I saw my beautiful grandma, she hugged me and told me she had been looking for me for a while. She explained how she flew in from California just for me. It brought back some good memories. I always loved my grandma. I remembered that she read Cat in the Hat stories to me and made me breakfast before school. When my parents were still in my life she used to give me money and take me and some of my friends out to eat. She even bought us some brand new Dickie pants. I hadn't felt that kind of love in years. She asked me how I was doing and I lied. I said I was ok. I was embarrassed to tell her how things went at home with my mom. I remember how much joy she had from seeing me and telling me she loved me and that she was going back to California.

My El Paso grandma, Rosemary Sandoval, also started looking for me and eventually got custody of me. So I ended up moving to the east side of El Paso. I had a place to stay again in my grandma's mobile home with Grandma Rosemary and my step-grandpa.

Man, was I messed up. I had become calloused around my heart and I know they saw that. My grandparents barely had enough to survive on and I ended up sharing a room with my uncle who lived with them too. This is the uncle whose wife had left with my dad to California. We were poor. Grandma always cooked beans - and burned the beans. The smoke alarm would go off and my grandma would yell my grandpa's name, saying she burned the beans again. My uncle used to get ten dollars' worth of food stamps a month. He was on disability so he would get a little bit of money. He smoked and still smokes to this day like a train. I remember him buying us beer or green Mickeys Malt Liquor bottles and boy did we have a good time drinking them. He would buy sardines that came in canned metal containers and when he would take them out to eat with me, it was as if we were eating a ribeye steak.

I started seeing my family a lot more. My other uncles, aunts and cousins were coming around. My uncles lived in some projects in the east side of El Paso. One of them had just gotten out of prison. My other uncles were old school gang members from the VNE gang on the northeast side of El Paso, which is a bad neighborhood. When I stayed with them I'd see more drugs than I ever had, even rooms full of marijuana bricks stacked to the ceiling. They would give me quarter pounds of weed for free. I thought I was the coolest kid because of who I was becoming and because I got free drugs. My uncles spray painted VNE, their street gang, really big on a rock wall in another gang's territory. You don't do that. It's considered disrespect, and usually starts a war. My uncles didn't care. The offended gang came and confronted them, and one of my uncles pulled out an AK 47 assault rifle. My other uncle that had just got out of prison told them, "The gang I roll with controls the El Paso streets." The other gang got so scared they didn't mention any more of it. I think they would rather have them as friends than enemies. They started hanging around with them and, in my eyes, trying to be like them. I was in awe of my uncles. I wanted to be just like them. These are the same uncles, my mom's brothers, who were going to kill my dad.

I got so drunk off hard liquor at that apartment that I would start throwing up in the toilet. The uncles laughed at me. One time I remember a gun pointed at my head. I was terrified as the trigger pulled. The gun had no bullets. They all thought it was funny. It was pretty crazy.

My uncle that had just gotten out of prison would wake up at 4:00 to 5:00 a.m. no matter how hard everyone had partied. He would wake up everyone else in the apartment and yell in Spanish, "Cleaning time!" We cleaned until everything was spotless.

One of my uncles and I revolted and locked the door in the room we were in. We slept late that day. It reminded me of the detention home. If you were a young inmate there you were made to clean and go to school whether you liked it or not. I thought that lifestyle was so ingrained into my uncles that it had become normal to them.

I can say this to all the kids out there reading this, if you don't know how to respect other people or help to learn to clean at your home, you will learn in detention if you choose to live a lifestyle like the one I lived. Whether you like it or not, you will be forced to. This doesn't come from the correction guards, but by the inmates doing time themselves.

I started going to middle school on the east side of El Paso. My grandparents were pastors and started telling me about this Jesus Christ character. They tried to tell me about Him all the time. I hated it. They preached to me while they were dropping me off at school or whenever they could. I thought they were crazy. I really didn't believe there was a God. My life was horrible. If there was a God, I thought, "Where is he?" Why would this loving God let all this happen in my life? Things didn't get better and were about to get a lot worse.

Getting ready for school meant putting on oldies or gangster rap. I listened to artists like Mary Wells, who is my favorite oldie singer, or rappers like Kid Frost, Dr. Dre, and Cypress Hill, Tupac, and artists of that sort. I ironed my Dickie pants, white shirts and checkered flannel jacket. If it was cold, I'd iron for like an hour straight and use starch so the creases would last all day. I can still probably iron better than a housewife. I would also use Tres Flores, a Mexican American gangster hair product, as far as I was concerned, to comb my hair slick back.

I would be ironing when my Grandma Rosemary would make coffee to wake up, and she would always make me a cup.

6.

Add Drugs

By the young age of twelve, I was already dabbling in selling drugs. One of the drugs I would buy and sell for double the price was roche pills, better known in America as the date rape drug.  My homeboys and I would not rape anyone – that was against our rules, but boy we would take them. I would take two or three roche pills with the cup of coffee Grandma made me before school every day. They would hit me almost instantly, within twenty minutes. The pills dissolved quicker than usual in the hot coffee, and on an empty stomach they would hit hard. I loved the feeling, and caffeine of any type intensified the effect when taking those types of pills.

I remember seeing on the news or meeting other people later on that would overdose or even die just by taking one or two of those pills. I'd laugh and think to myself, "What weak people."

I went to my first day of middle school and met a kid that asked me if I was new. I replied, "Yes." He was dressed just like me so I figured he came from a similar background. Boy was I wrong. We started hanging around. I remember a gang approached us.  I would eventually grow to hate that gang in those days, and it lasted for years. They came running up to us when we were walking home from school and they must have always picked on him because he got scared when he saw them. They asked me what gang I rolled with. I immediately answered, with boldness, "I'm from Westside Locos, Jackie's gang and where I'm from we would go at it at anytime, anywhere with any gang." I told my new, scared friend, "Get ready to throw down," which meant get ready to fight.  I looked around and saw a broken chain on the ground. I picked it up and wrapped it around my hand. My new friend told me he had a little knife on him, and I told him to pull it out and get ready to use it. He looked at me like I was crazy. I started heading towards these guys, ready to rumble, and they ran away scared. I laughed and yelled "Puro Westside Locos PvJ gang!"

The kid I was with was amazed by what I had done.  I walked him to his house. He had a beautiful house and a mom and a dad.  It freaked me out and I wondered why he was trying to live a gang member's lifestyle. He didn't have to live like that. In my mind he just wanted to be cool.  I found out later that the gang that approached us that day always picked on him and that this was their territory.

I started making friends in the mobile home park where I lived with my grandparents. There was one guy that lived right across the street. I started drinking beer and smoking weed with him. He must have been at least twenty-eight-years old.  I was only thirteen, but it wasn't anything new to me. That was normal back in Jackie's – hanging around guys that were way older than you. We would kick it together. He would get drunk and he'd tell me stories about how bad he was and how he had a reputation for being a thug. Even at thirteen, I knew he was a liar. We hung out together for years to come.

I learned in my previous neighborhood that you don't have to say a word or try to convince anyone how bad or how hardcore you are. People knew my uncles or my homeboys didn't have to say much and if you tried messing with those types of street guys you would find out quick what they were about. Real street guys didn't have to say much because they lived it.  People who talked too much or tried to convince you were usually fakes or liars who didn't understand that type of lifestyle.

Things didn't change much in middle school. I was always in trouble, always doing drugs and I started beating guys up from the east side gang that had hit me up and tried to scare me. I started beating them up so much that their older homeboys would actually come looking for me. They even came to the middle school at lunch time in cars packed with members of their gang, or after school when everyone would be getting out of school.

One of my uncles gave me a big buck knife, maybe seven or eight inches long. This particular uncle loves knives. Back in the day, when he was in his teens, he was known for stabbing rival gang members with the whole blade. He must have had at least thirty to fifty knives at the time, and he would sharpen the knives with different sharpening stones he had. He actually shaved with those knives! He gave me the knife to protect myself if I had to.

Two of my uncles used to talk to me about how to stab people. One would tell me, "I know the type of lifestyle you're going to live, so I'm gonna tell you this. If you're ever gonna rob someone, hold your blade where two or three inches are out and stab whoever you're robbing. If you're in a fight, you'll scare them from seeing their own blood, and if you're robbing someone they will see their blood and give you their money. It won't kill them and you won't get as much jail time. My second uncle told me not to listen to him. "You might as well stick the whole blade in whoever you're gonna stab." It was a trip having uncles like them.

Every weekend I would ride the city bus to the west side and kick it with all my home boys from Jackie's.

7.

Building Friendships

When I went to Jackie's on the weekends, more guys around my age or younger started hanging around with us. They either lived there or lived around the area of our territory. Homeboys like Barney who had moved to the Jackie's projects from another project on the west side with a gang who we considered enemies. My older homeboys really picked on him and beat him up a little bit more than the others because of it, but he got jumped into the gang and was down for our cause. Another homeboy that was younger than me was Tiny. He lived in the Jackie's projects. I don't ever remember him having his dad in his life. His mom was a drug dealer who sold marijuana, cocaine, and heroin. A lot of the homeboys would buy drugs from her. Tiny, even though he was younger than us, would always have drugs on him. Conejo, in English – Rabbit, moved to the Jackie's from some project in south central El Paso. I remember always picking on him and trying to fight with him.

We had big parties at Valdo and Manny's house. A lot of the homeboys from young to old would get together there, everyone drinking and doing drugs. We would fill the whole apartment up and it was no small apartment. It was an apartment with four floors. The guys my age would be partying on the first and second floor.

Valdo and Manny's mom and other old school homeboys such as Chuy, Spider, Joker, Speedy, Yogi and many others who were always in and out of jail or prison, played cards or dominoes, drank and did drugs on the third and fourth floor. Many times the guys would go up there with girls to have sex or chill out. Manny partied there with guys his age like Pee Wee and Koko.

We started to grow bigger and stronger. Even though I lived in the east side now, I considered the west side, Jackie's, my home. It was at this time that a lot of the homies from Jackie's really started getting into heroine. A lot of us kicked back at Barney's house, playing oldies in the background while they prepared the utensils ready to shoot heroine. They used a beer bottle cap and cotton from the inside of a cigarette butt, and placed black tar heroin inside that they usually purchased from Tiny's mom, or the Segundo Barrio in downtown El Paso. Then they put a little bit of water into the beer bottle cap and started heating it up with a lighter, and then mixed it with the back end of a syringe needle. They would stick the cotton into the bottle cap which would then absorb the water and the heroine. Then they used the needle from the syringe to suck up the heroine from the bottle cap and shoot it up into their veins. Sometimes they would mix cocaine in with the heroine and shoot it that way. They called it speed ball. They smoked weed, took pills, and drank beer all the time.

My homeboys got so messed up that many times they would have whole cigarettes hanging out of their mouths burned to nothing but ash, never having taken a hit. When the heroine would kick in, they would be telling each other "Orale" or "Qvole cakis" or "si me entiendes ese normal" - Mexican American gangster quotes in the hood. A lot of my homeboys lived to steal and get high.

 Not all of us, but some. I was a little bit different. I wanted to do drugs too, but I also wanted to be a drug dealer myself. I wanted to be either respected or feared. Now, I'm not saying my homeboys weren't down because they were. We were all crazy. They groomed us to be hard as nails. In my mind, there was no gang bigger or badder than ours, but I didn't want to be known as someone who just stole to get high. I wanted to control things like I had seen from the older homeboys and especially my uncles. If I stole or robbed a house it was to have money in my pocket, not just to be high. Don't get me wrong. I was always on drugs and high myself, but a hardcore respected or feared gangster is what I dreamed to be and I was headed straight towards that.

Back at school on the east side I was always in trouble. It was hard for my grandparents to control me. I wouldn't listen to them. I stayed out late and did whatever I wanted. I was not disrespectful to them in the sense that in those days, the early 1990s, gang members respected their elders. If we saw an older lady in the neighborhood carrying groceries into her home, we would ask if she needed help and help her. If I was ever caught cussing or being disrespectful to my grandparents and my uncles found out, I would get a beating. I never forgot. I just did whatever I wanted, and if they yelled or got mad at me I would just ignore them. It was looked down upon, in my day, to disrespect your elders.

I was always in so much trouble at school that that they put me in SAC, which was a place where they put troublemakers. You weren't allowed to eat with the other students at lunchtime, and we were pretty much stuck in that class room. I would be in there the whole day. Even there I wouldn't listen and I ended up in the BIC program again in middle school. This was for the worst kids. I hated the BIC program, and my grandparents were sick and tired of putting up with me.

I think my aunt and uncle in Las Vegas told my grandma to send me to them to see if I would act better.

8.


Las Vegas


Before I went to high school in El Paso, I ended up with my aunt, uncle, and cousins in Las Vegas, Nevada.  They had moved out there maybe a year earlier. That's where I got to see my older cousin Izzy again, the one who I liked being around and who taught me how to skateboard years earlier. He was there because he and his mom had issues themselves. He had been on his own since he was sixteen years old, and he was there working trying to save money and better himself.

We lived in an area knick-named "Naked City."  It was a bad area too.  My aunt enrolled me in a school there, but nothing really changed in my life for the months I stayed with them. I found little gang members to hang around with, and started smoking weed with them. I had to clean my aunt's house, and do other little chores. I slept on the living room couch because their two-bedroom apartment had barely enough space for my aunt, uncle and cousins. That was fine with me. It was better than living on the streets or at the detention home back in El Paso, and as long as I listened to basic rules, I was OK.

My uncle was one of the ones that wanted to kill my dad, but they always showed me love as I was a kid and had no fault in what my dad did. He was strict about keeping his rules. My uncle was a hard core guy who everyone respected in the streets, and someone I looked up to.  I had parties there and got drunk and made my little cousins fight the other little kids in the neighborhood just to entertain Izzy and me. Since we didn't have boxing gloves for them, we would wrap towels or bed sheets around their little hands and make them fight. I loved being around my older cousin and family.

My aunt and uncle started having personal problems and divorced, so I ended up back at Grandma Rosemary's mobile home in El Paso. I was fourteen-years-old and getting ready to start school at Hanks High School in the east side of El Paso.

You'd think it couldn't get worse, but it did.

9.

Back to El Paso

Before I moved to Las Vegas, I had met a few friends that lived in Grandma Rosemary's mobile home park. One of them was a white kid named Devin who was from Cleveland, Ohio. He was my only white friend from back in the day that would hang around with me and knew how crazy I was. We always smoked weed or took pills, or did acid at his house. He had an uncle named Juan he often told me about. Juan was married to his aunt. He was Mexican American like me and must have been around twenty-eight at the time. He had just gotten out of prison and was from a notorious prison gang. That gang was a stronghold in San Antonio, TX and Los Angeles CA.

Devin was a tagger not a gang member. A tagger is someone more interested in creating graffiti than gang banging. I used to hang around with him once in a while and met all his tagger friends. They all told me about this notorious Juan. The day came when I finally met him. He grew up crazy like me and was a big time drug dealer. Juan and I hit it off. He liked me a lot since I was crazy too. He used to slap and intimidate Devin's tagger friends. You could tell they were scared, intimidated, or respected Juan a lot. So we started hanging around with each other drinking alcohol, taking roche pills together or smoking weed. We got along pretty well and started doing drug deals together.

It was normal at that point for me to sell drugs, but I was into pills or marijuana in small portions. That all changed when I met Juan. Through him I made connections buy and sell quarter pounds of weed, and then pounds. Grandma Racheal from California would send me twenty to thirty bucks every other week, so I would steal and save the money she sent me until I'd saved around seventy bucks. Back then I could buy a quarter pound of weed for sixty to seventy bucks, and sell it to make around $140 to $200. I was learning the drug trade business and eventually bought pounds of weed and made more money.

This all took place before I started high school. On the first day of high school, I met other gang members from the east side Sherman gang. I met a guy nicknamed Flaco, and we got along great. We had the same enemies. We both didn't like the gang that I used to fight in middle school by myself, so we hit it off. We smoked some weed together, and he showed me the ropes. He showed me where certain people hung out and where to buy drugs. He introduced me to the different gangs in the area. Flaco's gang controlled that area like my gang Jackie's controlled ours on the west side. I also met another tagger nicknamed Index. His tagging crew got along with Flaco and his gang so we all started hanging around together. We didn't care much for going to school. We met to sell drugs, meet girls, start fights, gang bang and make money. We were always ditching school to go parties, either at Flaco's or some homeboy's apartment. There was beer, drugs and girls, or fights.

I partied with Index. He had a car with a big speaker system. Loud bass boomed from the trunk. In those days the louder your radio sound system the cooler you were. Everyone wanted to hang around you, especially if you had drugs, which we always had. We were straight up little hustlers and thugs making a name for ourselves.

10.

Mexico

So at fourteen-years-old my life consisted of waking up, drinking coffee with the roche pills after ironing my clothes. Index would pick me up in his car to supposedly "study" and do well at school, which was a joke. We really went to go to school to sell drugs, gang bang, and fight and make money. I made probably $200 to $400 a day at that age. We started going to different high schools throughout El Paso to sell weed, and we realized that everyone asked for roche pills. I purchased my pills from the Segundo Barrio in El Paso and I started buying so many that one of the old school guys told me "Hey, Huero, why don't you go to Juarez, buy them there and just walk back from Mexico to El Paso. They named a few pharmacies that would sell them to us.

Mexico really has no law. Even if cops stop you and you have illegal drugs on you, all you have to do is pay them off. So that's exactly what we did. We stopped getting the pills from the Segundo Barrio. We got them direct from a source at a pharmacy in Juarez. We would park the car on the American side of El Paso in the downtown area and walk across the border into Mexico. We searched the pharmacies for the best deal. They knew exactly what we were doing. We found a pharmacy that would sell them for ten cents a pill as long as we were buying two bottles or more. Each bottle contained ninety roche pills, so two bottles would equal to one hundred eighty pills.

In those days it was common for kids from El Paso to cross into Mexico and go to bars to drink. The eight dollar cover charge was named "drink and drown." Eight dollars for all you could drink. So high school kids would have ditching parties in Mexico and get drunker than drunk. Throughout the years I partied in Mexico many times. The first time I went drinking in Mexico I was nine or ten years old. I would go either with my gang or with my older cousin Izzy.

Going to Mexico was nothing new to me, but this was a little different because we could get busted coming back to America with illegal drugs. Getting caught would mean a good chunk of time behind bars. So we emptied the pills out of the bottle and I would stick some, wrapped in plastic they'd given us at the pharmacy, into each one of my shoes at the very tips. I would cut a small incision in my boxer shorts, pants and jacket if it was cold, and wrap a ball of them under each arm pit. The lady at the pharmacy would tape them so they wouldn't fall out before I crossed the border.

We bought about six bottles our first time. The lady said, in Spanish, "Be careful, Mijo I'll be waiting to see you soon." I remember taking like eight roche pills with a Coca Cola to get blitzed. I thought, "If they catch me, at least I'll be messed up. My friends only took like two or three, saying, "You're crazy." Back across the border we went to the American side where border patrol and drug sniffing dogs were. I thought "I hope the dogs don't sniff the pills on me." It would be a long jail sentence. But the border patrol agents were walking around with dogs, which is a normal at any border crossing from Mexico into America. When the border patrol agents passed by me with the dogs, nothing happened. As time went on we started crossing the border with roche pills every day or every other day.

I think pills are considered a legal drug if you have a prescription. U.S. Citizens were allowed to get pills at a discounted price in Mexico and cross them legally if you declared them as you crossed. Of course roche pills were not legal, but we found a loophole in the system and used it to the fullest. I believe their dogs were trained to sniff marijuana, cocaine or heroin, drugs of that sort, so you did not get searched unless you acted worried or suspicious. Don't get me wrong - Juarez, Mexico was a very dangerous place to be doing what we were doing, but my lifestyle in general was dangerous so it really didn't faze me. Walking through the streets of Juarez was crazy, but crazy is how I lived and I loved it. Most people who say they've changed their life for good will usually say they hated how they used to live, but not me.

I was addicted to living crazy.

11.

## Death Wish

Most who knew me at that age say I had a death wish, which was kind of true. I didn't value my life at all. I started making even more money, eating where I wanted, bought the clothes I wanted, and bought gold chains and watches. I partied as much as I wanted, and if sometimes I spent all my money it didn't matter. I would just steal some more and buy more drugs to sell and have money anyways.

I was very hurt in my life, but I learned to channel the hurt into hate and anger. That's one of the reasons I think I didn't like school. I saw parents cheering their kids at sports events, and just being involved in their lives. It made me furious. I would think how my life would have been so different if I had my parents involved that way. I remember cutting my wrists, trying to commit suicide. I still have scars on my wrists to this day.

Let me just stop here for a moment and say to whoever is feeling suicidal as I did at this early age. You'll see through the story you're about to read that your life is going to get better. Don't give in or give up. Life might seem as if there's no hope, but trust me - there is hope. I hope that by reading my story you will be encouraged to not give in to a lie. There is so much more in life. Things will change and get better. There is always hope. I know what you're feeling and what you're going through. You have to keep keeping on. Sometimes in life you just have to put one foot in front of the other until change comes and you see your life get better. You will not regret living. Life has great things in store for you. Trust me when I tell you - there is hope in your future. Don't give in. More people love you than you think. Don't hurt yourself or others around you. Whether you're dealing with bullying, drug addiction or sickness, or you're just plain depressed, there is hope ahead. Give life a chance because great things await you in your beautiful future.

I was either high, out of my mind on drugs, self-medicating myself, or I was miserable and angry at the world. I blamed a lot of those feelings on my parents.

The teachers, security guards, and principals started putting a lot of their focus on me. They knew through student informants that I was one of the major drug dealers at school. It didn't help that I hung around other known gang members. I was always in trouble at the office for gang banging and being in fights against gangs I considered to be enemies. They were always checking me and padding me down for drugs. I knew I was on their radar. I would use creative, ingenious ways to make sure I never got caught with drugs on me.

My Jackie's home boys and I hid drugs in brick or rock walls. We loosened bricks from the wall and hid drugs behind the brick. This was something I saw the drug dealers do in the Segundo Barrio. They also had look-outs on each corner and yelled "Cops!" or whistled to warn the other dealers so no one would have drugs on them and get busted.

I used that tactic with marijuana. I hid it outside of the school at places only I knew. For the roche pills, I carried an ultra-big fat permanent marker around. After opening the marker I would stick some tissue paper at the bottom of the open marker and push it as hard as I could, then put a little piece of plastic on top of the tissue paper so the ink from the marker wouldn't bleed through onto the pills. I would put them into the back onto the end of the marker, and then I would stuff more tissue paper on top of the pills and then put the cap back onto the end of the marker. That way, even if anyone shook the marker, you could not hear anything. You'd just think it was a marker.

Tagging and gang graffiti was a big thing in those days. A lot of teenagers carried markers around and all they would do if they got caught with one is take the marker away. I had many taken away and it hurt me every time because I lost money, but at least I wasn't getting busted for drugs and going to jail.

Yet.

12.

## Growing the Gang

Back in the Jackie's projects, when I was around fifteen, we really started growing. There was a big gang named Diablo, the DDT gang, in south central El Paso. A lot of them ended up moving to the Jackie's projects or area because their housing projects were being torn down by the city. The Diablo gang did not get along with our best known rivals on the West side. We made an alliance with the Diablos. We let them hang out with us at the Jackie's projects as long as they understood whose territory they were in, respect it, and absolutely no spray painting their gang graffiti on our walls. A few of them actually grew up in Jackie's so we knew some of them since elementary school.

One time my younger homeboys and a few my age came running up to me in the desert behind Jackie's where I was hanging out. They came to me saying "The guys from Diablo are here in a limousine!"

I said "OK, so what's going on?" My homeboys made it seem like they had come to start trouble so I asked them, "Who else is here in the hood?"

They said, "No one's here. We think everyone's partying in Juarez."

I said, "Well let's go hit 'em up." I always made it a point to show the younger ones to control our area with an iron fist. A few weeks earlier some of the younger homeboys came to the projects from a few blocks up. They said they'd been driving by a street we controlled and a known member from a rival gang started throwing gang signs up at them. There were maybe six to seven of my younger homeboys in a blue pickup truck and I said, "Let's go back up there." I was infuriated that they didn't beat him up while driving up the street. I saw there was a bat in the back of the truck.

When we got to the apartment where the rival gang member lived, I got down and knocked on his door. His parents were saying, "Please leave, he's not here." I knew they were lying so I started busting all their windows with the bat, yelling for him to come out.   Of course he never did and his mom and dad and everyone else in the house was yelling, scared. After busting all their windows and trying to kick their front door open, we got back to the Jackie's projects and I started going off on my little homies telling them let it be known we control this area. We never let anyone disrespect us.

That's why they wanted me to go with them when the guys from Diablo came in the big white limo. But when I got there, there was no problem. My homeboy Junior came out of the limo and was all messed up saying, "Hey, que rollo, Huero," and some of his other homeboys came out of the limo saying "Hey, we're cool with Jackie's. We respect your turf and mean no disrespect."  So, all was good.  Junior and I started hanging around a lot. He would throw big parties at his apartment in the Jackie's and a few guys from the Diablos would be there, but really it would be jam packed with Jackie's homeboys and homegirls our age. Junior and I knew each other since elementary, so we were cool. Junior started hanging around with us so much I guess he figured he might as well be part of our gang, and since their projects had been torn down, they were always kicking it with us.

One night after a party at Junior's house, it was just me and him there talking, getting high and drunk, and he said, "Hey, Huero, I want to be part of the Jackie's gang and I said, "OK, tomorrow we will jump you in." At this time there were a lot more guys our age in the gang so he wanted to be jumped in with a few others our age. I agreed, but I lied.

I told some old schoolers Junior wanted to get jumped in. I figured I got jumped in, no different, why shouldn't he? So the next day me, Cruz, and our older homeboy Chuy jumped Junior in. We were beating him up for a while and the only reason we stopped is because Chuy body slammed him on a parked car in Jackie's, and the car alarm turned on. I remember we nicknamed Junior Indio. He couldn't walk for three days from the beating he received.  I knew we would grow stronger and that the rest of the guys from Diablo that hung around Jackie's would soon follow Indio's footsteps and join our gang. Indio was looked up to by them and they all did get into Jackie's except one, but he would still hang around with us.  We were growing and becoming more powerful and the guys who got into Jackie's from Diablo were as down and crazy as we were. I couldn't be happier.

We grew so much that we were filling Indio's four-story apartment with more people our age. Our parties were better than the old schooler's parties now. Sometimes the older guys would come over wanting to party with us and all the girls we had. They would come over and knock on Indio's door and window wanting to come in, and we would look through the window and laugh at them. Boy, would they get mad! They would start cussing at us and tell us they were gonna beat us up and we would laugh at them. We didn't really care if they beat us up. We were used to it. The difference between our parties and theirs were that ours were loud. Everyone enjoyed themselves. We had loud music, either oldies or gangster rap and theirs were quiet, everyone all serious because they had all pretty much been to prison. As a matter of fact if you talked too much or made too much noise or wanted to blast the radio, you would likely get beaten up. So we didn't want them messing up our parties or have to go by their stupid prison rule. That's at least how we thought back then.

I remember not seeing my homeboy Tiny at the parties so much anymore, and we found out he, at eleven-years-old, had gotten his fourteen-year-old girlfriend pregnant. It was a trip! When Tiny's baby was born, me and my homeboys would be walking by his apartment and see him out there with his girlfriend and a stroller with his newborn baby in it. We would be on our way to steal and party and to me he looked hilarious. Tiny would be there, dressed in his Dickies, muscle shirt and Nike Cortez shoes. He shaved his head totally bald but left a long pony tail on the back of his head. Tiny was my younger homeboy and I was one of the ones that schooled him in our ways. I made fun of him and gave him hell because of his situation. Tiny was always down and ready to roll with us wherever we went, but his girlfriend would tell him, "Stay with me," and "Your baby don't go hang out with your friends." So on purpose we would force him to go with us and harass him until he did. I can remember his girlfriend with a sad look on her face when we would take Tiny with us, but we didn't care. We didn't know any better.

Back on the east side, at my grandma's house, my sister showed up with all her belongings. I found out she was not getting along with my mom. I guess after I was gone my mom started taking out her anger on my little sister and ended up kicking her out. So she started hanging around with me and my east side homeboys. I was very protective of my baby sister. I would kind of take care of her like I was a father to her so all my homeboys always respected her and took care of her as well.

My homeboys from Jackie's started coming to the east side and visiting me at my grandma's mobile home. I remember when they first started coming over they would trip out and tell me, "Hey Huero, this looks like it's our turf."  The reason they said that is because all around the east side you could see big old spray painted block letters that were all colored in with spray paint on lots and lots of the walls all over saying "Jackie's" or "PvJ WSL Huero." The gang that I fought in on the east side would also have spray paint all over walls there as it was their territory. You could see their gang's spray paintings crossed out with a big X,  then my graffiti right next to theirs showing I was the one who did it. That is a sign of disrespect in gang culture, and it usually meant if either were crossing each other out on walls, there would be problems if they ran into each other. I just didn't care. I was wild and out of control. I laughed and told my homeboys, "This is our turf," then they laughed and said it looked like our turf.  By then I always carried a knife or a big screwdriver like ten inches long to stab anyone who wanted problems with me or my gang. My friends tripped out on me, but they themselves were just as crazy.

This one particular time Valdo, Indio, Cruz, Tiny, Conejo were driving a brand new Jeep when they pulled up to my grandma's mobile home. I was outside doing a drug deal and they rolled up in and yelled out the window, "What's up, Huero?" I went up to the Jeep window and saw my homeboys inside. I said exactly what I was thinking.

"Where you steal this Jeep from?"

Valdo said, "I didn't steal it, I bought it - cash."  I remember laughing, saying, "Yeah right," and Valdo pulled the keys out of the ignition and wiggled the keys in my face.  My next question was "How'd you buy it?"

My homeboy Indio held up kilos of marijuana and cocaine saying, "Get in, let's go party."

I was with an ex-girlfriend of mine and I said, "Alright, let me go tell this chick I'm jamming out with, you guys." She made such a big deal about me leaving so I told them to turn the Jeep around towards the street so we could leave.  I told the girl, "I'm going to tell my friends I can't go," because this girl started hugging on me, not wanting to let me go. I said, "I'll be right back." I walked up to the Jeep and I told my homeboys to open the door, and when they did I jumped in and closed the door. The girl chased the Jeep yelling cuss words at me. Valdo put the pedal to the metal as we all laughed at her. Man, we partied hard. We ended up with some different girls at some projects in the northeast side of El Paso where my uncles were from.

Indio pulled out a big wad of money. Before we arrived, we'd made a beer run. We all got out at a corner convenient store and all of us grabbed two 18 packs of Budweiser beer each. After that we headed to the apartment on the northeast side, ready to party. Even though we all had money, we were underage and were not legally able to buy beer. We'd have stolen it anyway. It's just the way we lived. So at the apartment Indio gave me cocaine non-stop for three days. We partied so hard, I didn't get back home to my grandma's for a week.

Boy, were we crazy.

13.

Building My Rep

On the east side, my reputation was pretty notorious for beating people up, robbing people, houses, and selling drugs. I met true, old school gangsters and hung around them. Isaiah Blancas - a real street guy, as hard core as they came. If someone looked at me second too long, I'd start trouble with you.  The beating would be so bad that my victims would be shaking and convulsing on the floor. I thrived on stuff like that. I loved seeing blood.

I'd become the respected and feared gang member that I always wanted to be.

If you weren't from my gang, or I didn't know you or respect you, I was a nightmare of an adversary to have.  You didn't want to test to see if I was really down in the lifestyle. In my mind, I was living to the fullest. Many friends or people that remember me or hung around me from back in the day would tell you the exact same thing. They would tell you I had a death wish, which at that point I think I did. I really didn't care about life anymore. I had already accepted my outcome, which comes with living a street life. Either I was going to die in the streets from drugs or face a life imprisonment term.

One of the old school gangsters I hung with was named Bam Bam. He had a pool table in his garage, and old school hardcore gangsters would hang out there drinking hard liquor and doing drugs. Bam Bam was a respected O.G. (Original Gangster) prison gang member, and drug dealer. I liked hanging around him. I think he would trip out on me because I was young, but really crazy. We got along. He schooled me in the gangster ways. He also knew my uncles and they had respect towards one another, and I respected Bam Bam.

One particular night I was there kicking back with him and a lot of his homeboys were there. At that time I was taking around forty to eighty roche pills a day. I popped those puppies as if I was eating M&Ms

candies. As a matter of fact, a lot of my homeboys from Jackie's were full blown heroin addicts, and when I would party with them, I would sell them big quantities. I gave drugs to them nonstop, and they got so messed up after taking like ten to sixteen roche pills that they couldn't hang with me. That's how much tolerance I had built up to drug use. I started drinking hard liquor too. I began mixing and matching drugs at a whole new level.

I was just there enjoying myself at Bam Bam's when one of his homeboys kept looking at me – I stared right back at him. Most kids my age would have been scared out of their minds, but not me. I kept looking right back at him, mad-dogging him. It's a term we used when we looked at someone with not-so-good intentions.

"What are you looking at, Pee Wee?" he asked. Pee Wee is what old school gangsters called youngsters living crazy.

My respect for Bam Bam kept me from asking the same thing. Bam Bam always told me I was welcome as long as I respected his house didn't start problems. I was just waiting for this gangster to say something. I always carried my big knife or screwdriver with me. It was lodged at an angle down my Dickie pants under my shirt.

"I'm looking at you," I said, in not so nice words, and I was heading towards him. I intended to stab him right there on the spot, but as I walked across the room, Bam Bam stopped me.

"Come, here, little homie. Let's have a talk." He said, "Homito, this is my house, I got love for you but you can't do that here."

I got mad and tried to justify myself. "He started it."

He said, "Look, little homie, you probably, more than likely, are going to be rolling with the same prison gang we roll with. Let's go back in and kick it, and respect my house.

I said, "Ok, I will, but he better not look at me no more." So back into his garage we went. I think the guy knew I was a crazy little hot-head that wasn't scared of him and would go all out.

The rest of the night I hung out, and for hours I was mad-dogging that old schooler on purpose. I was still mad and wanted to stab him. He wouldn't even look my way anymore. I think he knew I wanted to really do him harm and he left the party early.

14.

Ink Tough

Around this time I also started getting tattoos. A few of my uncles did prison style tattoos. They made handmade tattoo guns and used guitar string as the needle. I got small tattoos in Jackie's when I was younger, like the three dots on your wrist that meant 'Mi Vida Loca' (My Crazy Life). Along with my homeboy Valdo I also had tattooed WSL on my leg, and a cross with two dots on my other leg, and four dots between my shoulder and chest. It was just me and my friends being crazy.

Those tattoos were done between the ages of nine and twelve, but I wanted my uncle to tattoo a PvJ tattoo in old English letters between my shoulder blades on my back to show my allegiance to my gang, so I got my first real tattoo. My uncles poured tequila over the tattoo when they were finished and slapped the area with their hand. I witnessed this when they were free and not locked up.

My uncles, as I've stated before, were real street guys. I had uncles on my mom's side and dad's side of my family that have spent over thirty years of their lives behind bars.

I eventually got another two tattoos on both my upper arms.

I met a guy nicknamed Tiny from the LFL gang, which was another big gang in El Paso. We got along. Tiny's dad was well respected in the streets. He was in the same prison gang my friend Devin's uncle Juan was from.

Tiny was covered in tattoos from his fingers to his neck. We got to talking quite a bit and I found out that Tiny actually lived in the Jackie's area when he was younger and went to the same elementary school. He explained how his own dad had tattooed him and all his brothers and sisters since they were really young. I remembered seeing him in elementary when we were younger, and I started laughing.

"I remember you. You would dress all gangstered out with a flannel shirt where just the very top button on the shirt would be buttoned.

Your sleeves would be rolled up with all your tattoos showing, and you would always walk around with your arms around two girls,."

He said, "Yeah, that was me." We both started laughing. Tiny offered to tattoo me for free, so I went to his house and met his dad who was also called Tiny. When I walked into their house, his dad said to me, "Que rollo, what's up?"

I said "Orale que rollo," back to him. I was drunk and messed up on roche pills and high on weed. So Tiny, even though he was fifteen, he already knew how to do tattooing. His dad had trained him since he was a kid. He pulled out a homemade tattoo gun, like the tattoo guns my uncles used. He asked me what I wanted tattooed on me.

"I want a PvJ in old English letters on my arm. Under the PvJ I want it to spell out West Side in old English letters also."

He said, "Orale, let's get down." I took off my shirt. I'd brought a bottle of hard liquor with me so I could drink while getting my new gang tattoo. We both sat down in his kitchen. I remember I faced his refrigerator and on the refrigerator door was a little magnet mirror. I could see his dad through it. He was checking out his son's art and he was drinking shots of the hard liquor I had brought with me. They had oldies playing in the background. Tiny's dad nodded at him and every time I would see him nodding, little Tiny would push the needle into my arm harder.

After a few times of seeing this, I stood up. "I don't care if you put the whole needle in my arm; just make sure the tattoo looks right when you're finished." His dad smiled and then started laughing. He said, "You're a down little homie, Huero." We all started laughing. His dad liked me. He knew I was down. It's funny, because after that he would invite me over a lot to hang out.

Not too long after that, I was there and a big guy a few years older than me went over to pay for a tattoo, and the same thing happened. Little Tiny's dad was nodding to push the needle in this guy's arm, but this guy receiving the tattoo started complaining and whining about it. Tiny's dad started beating this guy up real bad and kicked him out of his house. They didn't even finish his tattoo, and we all laughed. I guess he would test people by doing this. That's what made him like me so much - because I didn't care either, and lived crazy myself. I also tattooed PVJ on my finger at a party in Jackie's along with many of my homeboys.

15.

Deeper Darkness

Another crazy thing that I did around this point in my life was getting hooked up with a homeboy named Mando. He was a few years older than me. I met him in middle school on the east side at the BIC program for the worst of the worst kids. We hooked up three years after I met him in middle school. I was fifteen so he would've been around seventeen.

Back in middle school Mando would try to talk to me by our teacher's request. The teacher liked him and would ask him to talk to me about bettering myself. The truth was that Mando was just like me. When we hooked back up together years later it would be by drug dealing, drinking alcohol, and doing drugs together. Mando dressed just like me and my homeboys. He shaved his head bald, wore Dickie pants and white shirts with Nike Cortez. One thing I also remember about Mando is he always had cigarette burns on his forearm. He would put cigarettes out by pushing them right on his forearm. He always had scabs from doing that.

Not too much later on I found out why. We were partying hard one time. Mando knew I was crazy and he really liked that about me, so this particular time he invited me over to his apartment in the east side where he lived with his mom. Mando and his mom would sell pounds of marijuana and other drugs together. All three of us were partying hard, and I remember it must have been around two or three a.m. I would never have imagined in my wildest dreams what he was about to reveal. He asked me if I knew why he burned cigarettes off on his arm and of course I replied that I had no idea.

"Huero, I like you because you don't care about anything just like me. What I'm about to tell you I have told very few. Do you believe in Satan, the devil?"

I laughed and said, "I don't believe in God, Jesus, Satan, or the devil."

"Me and my mom worship Satan. Why do you think I'm so respected and sell all these drugs? I sell and never get caught. Satan protects me and gives me everything I want. I made a pact with the devil, and he told me he will give me power and everything I want or desire in this life. But at a certain age I will die, but I will have rank in hell when I die, when my soul is in hell. That's why I shave my head."

His mom was there and she explained how she served Satan too. It's at this time he asked me if he gave me a pound of marijuana, would I take a leap of faith and shave my head and repeat a prayer after him. He explained he believed I was one of the devil's chosen ones and Satan would give me money, drugs, women, and anything I wanted in this lifetime.

My eyes lit up. "You'll give me a pound of weed if I sell my soul?"

He said, "Yes, but you have to take it serious."

I said, "Sold. Let's do this." I really didn't believe in the devil or God. I didn't care to sell my soul. In my mind, I was getting a free pound of dope. So he got out shaving cream and razors to shave my head bald. I remember him turning some kind of candle on that he said represented some type of evil and before he started shaving my head I said "Give me my pound."

He brought it out to me and handed it to me. I was ecstatic. I thought, "This guy is giving me a pound of weed to accept the devil who I don't believe in." I couldn't have been happier. We went to his restroom and he started shaving my head. He'd brought that candle with him, and started rubbing what I thought was alcohol on my head. I really don't know what it was, even now. He pulled out a book and asked me to repeat after him, so I did. I left his place with my pound, but before I left he told me, "Don't ever tell anyone I worship the devil."

I said, "I won't." I was happy I had gotten free drugs. After this happened, I started putting cigarettes out on my arms. I must have had fifteen cigarette burns on my forearm in a straight line. I didn't do it because they were souls for the devil like Mando did. I just liked the pain. I had scars on my wrists from when I was suicidal when I was younger, and big old scabs on my arm now, too. People used to trip out on me. I got crazier than ever, though after doing that at Mando's, I became more violent. I was beating people up for no reason, and started robbing people and stealing on a whole new level. I also started stabbing members of enemy gangs I didn't get along with.

I remember going to get some roche pills from a homeboy supplier I used when I hadn't gone to Juarez. He and I would hook each other up with good drug deals. I was so messed up on drugs and alcohol that when I met him for the pills, I pulled out my screwdriver full of old blood from stabbing people. The screwdriver actually looked rusted, but it was just dry blood. He wanted no part of me. He tripped out so much that he just handed me a hundred pills wrapped in plastic, and said, "I'll give them to you, just leave, please."

I laughed and called him a little girl. He gave them to me free, and you could see the terror in his eyes. I went home to my grandma's mobile home, probably around 4:00 pm, and I was so high I told her jokingly, "I sold my soul to the devil. A friend of mine offered me some money to sell my soul and I took it.

Grandma Rosemary said, "You're playing, right?"

I said, "No, I'm not playing."

She got really mad. "Get in the car. I'm taking you to a church right now to get prayer."

"Come on, Grandma, you're tripping."

She made me go. When we got to the church, people were singing and praising God. Grandma went straight up to talk to the pastor. It must have been a friend of my grandparents as they were pastors too. The pastor called me up and she and many people laid hands on me, praying. It was weird to me because I felt this peace come over me as they were praying. I actually felt good.

As we were leaving the church, and I kid you not, as soon as I walked out of the church doors I got so sick I felt like I was dying. Grandma took me to the hospital and I had a 106° fever and I couldn't even drink water or hold anything in my stomach. I felt so bad that I thought I would rather die than feel the pain I was feeling. The doctor prescribed medicine and I went home. My fever would not go down for days. I couldn't even eat soup. Three days later I was rolling on the floor in agonizing pain.

Two weeks passed before I could finally hold water and soup in my stomach. The whole time my grandma was telling me about this Jesus Christ. I was so sick I really didn't care what anyone was telling me. When I felt better I had to admit what happened was very strange, but I still didn't serve or believe in this Jesus character.

I spiraled into even deeper darkness.

16.

## Down and Crazy

At this point in my life, a lot of my homeboys had already died from gang violence or drug overdoses. I remember thinking I wouldn't live to see seventeen because I was one of the worst ones. I had made so many enemies from either beating people up or stabbing them that gangs would actually go looking for me in cars filled with gang members. They intended to hurt or kill me if they could.

One time a car pulled up in front of me and the guys asked if I was Huero, and I replied, "I'm Huero from West Side Locos PvJ."

The supposed hardest gang member came out of the car saying his nickname and gang. I knew it well. I would slap them at parties around El Paso and go to their projects and spray paint my nickname and gang over their project walls and beat them up anywhere I would see them. So this guy came out with a crowbar and I think he expected me to get scared and run, but I was not the type to run from a fight. I had built my reputation by never backing down, even if ten guys were coming against me. In my mind, even if you beat me up and I at least get to stab two or three of you, I still won. So instead of running, I pulled out the big knife I always carried and headed straight towards him. He threw his crowbar down and ran back to the car.

I laughed and was screaming, "West Side Jackie's!" as I threw rocks at their car. El Paso is a city in the desert and you can find rocks almost anywhere. It was a normal thing in Jackie's to pile rocks at certain areas to use if enemy gangs cruised by and we didn't have guns on us. We would break their windows with the rocks we'd piled up. If we could rock their vehicles well enough and they'd have to stop, we'd beat them until they were unconscious or shaking and bleeding.

Another incident is when I was walking after school with the guys from east side Sherman to their projects. A car filled with enemy gang members pulled up on us. We couldn't have been but a few blocks from the high school. These guys that pulled up asked, "Where you from?"

I said, "West Side Locos," and the guys from Sherman said, "Sherman." I remember the guys in the car were looking for us. They had bandannas covering their faces. Two or three guns came out of the car windows and they started shooting at us. We dropped flat on the ground as I had done many times before, the only difference was this time they were shooting at me from only fifteen feet away. When the car sped off, I got up and checked my arms and the rest of my body for bullet holes or blood. Amazingly, I had not been shot. I thought they must have been using blanks, so I tried to throw rocks at the speeding car.

I later found out they used real bullets because someone had given some of our names to the cops, and when I arrived home to my grandma's house later on, the cops were there waiting for me. They wanted information on the shooters. Of course I told them nothing. It is a street code never to rat on anybody or ever cooperate with any type of law enforcement at any time. In my day, you would get a green light put on you if you did. You'd get a death sentence, stabbing or a severe beating. Real street guys never ratted or gave info to police. That's just how it was. I had a good clue who had shot at me and I was already planning revenge. My grandma told me later on in life that she was scared to answer her phone. She said she didn't know if I'd be in jail or dead. She would even freak out if the school called her as I was always in trouble.

I often saw a lot of my homeboys from Jackie's in downtown El Paso when I went out there to do drug deals or cross roche pills from Mexico. We would run into each other at the Placita downtown at the main bus terminal. This is where I saw PeeWee for the last time. He asked me if I had a joint, and I said I didn't. He took a bus going from the Placita to the Jackie's projects and he shot some dope up in the bus, overdosed and died. The bus driver found my friend dead. Pee Wee wasn't going to be the last friend I lost to drugs or gang violence. It became normal to me and my homeboys from Jackie's to hear of a friend's death. Sad but true.

I started getting into more and more trouble. Enemy gangs and law enforcement were always on me. I was talking to Grandma Racheal from California on the telephone, who I loved very much. My grandma's are my heroes. They were the closest thing I had to a mother and father. Grandma Racheal always asked me to go live with her so I said jokingly, "If you wire me 300 dollars for the plane ticket, I'll buy it and head my way over there." She actually sent me the money, but I had no intention of going. When the funds were available for pick up, I was partying at the east side Sherman projects with some homeboys there, and we went to pick up the money. I bought an 8 ball of cocaine, hard liquor, beer, and weed with the money. I didn't speak to my grandma for days. When I finally did, she asked if I had got the airplane ticket. I told her, "I need another 150 dollars, so send it." When I picked up the money, I bought a quarter pound of weed and hard liquor and partied even more. I started doing any and all kinds of drugs. I traded other well known drug dealers' roche pills for acid sheets.

I really loved LSD. I took anywhere from seven to fifteen little paper tabs that were soaked in LSD. You had to handle the sheets very carefully. I would grab the sheet of thick paper drenched in LSD with foil paper. If you touched the sheet of paper with the LSD in it, you could go on a permanent trip or overdose. I knew many who had tripped on too much acid and stayed crazy. You would see them walking around like zombies, talking to themselves. I surely didn't want to be living the lives they were. I'm not saying I didn't overdo acid myself because I did. I abused all drugs. I cut the acid sheets into little square papers that fit right on your finger tip, but I sold the little paper tabs wrapped in foil to keep its potency for customers. I always traded pills with guys that had the best acid out there. Another thing that amped up your high when you were taking acid was orange juice. Many I knew would just drink orange juice with some weed smoking going on. I even took that to another level. I would take my acid with orange juice mixed with Md 20/20, a hard liquor drink, and smoke weed along with it.

I tripped hard.

17.

California Kind of Crazy

Grandma Racheal called me once more to ask if I had bought my ticket to California and I said, "No." By this time she knew I was lying and said, "I'm buying your ticket and you're coming to California," and I said, "OK." I had been in nonstop trouble ending up at the detention home a lot, and I had new charges that were probably going to become warrants, so I figured it couldn't hurt to go cool out in California for a little while. Before I left and was packing my bags, I figured I would take two big packages of roche pills with me along with some weed. I took the soles of the inside of my shoes out, smashed two bags of weed until it was pretty flat, then stuck a whole bunch of peanut butter around both bags of compressed weed, then wrapped them both with plastic zip lock bags. I placed the bags in the shoes I was using to smuggle the weed, then placed the soles back into the shoes. I did the same thing to the roche pills, but instead of using shoes for the pills I stuffed them into socks and put more socks around them.

I was off to California. My dad, who I hadn't seen since he left, was picking me up from the Oakland California airport. I wasn't too excited about that. I was still mad about everything and had bottled anger and hate towards him and my mother. I couldn't wait to give him a piece of my mind.

The flight tripped me out. I was amazed by all the green trees, and I was also tripping out on the ocean. You didn't see that in El Paso. I thought it was pretty cool. The plane finally landed and I was in California.

My grandma lived on the Burlingame side of San Francisco. My dad lived in Hayward, California, which was on the Oakland side, and ghetto to the max. I was going to stay with him for a few months, but I loved it because of all the beautiful green trees and the ocean. I loved the fact that it was ghetto, too. It was just like my neighborhood back in El

Paso - spray paint on the walls and gangsters everywhere. I said to myself, "I'm going to have a good time out here."

As Dad was driving me to his place, I told him stop at the store to pick up some quarts of Mickeys Malt Liquor. When he got back into the vehicle I was already pulling out roche pills from my luggage. I would always throw like five roche pills into quarts and drink them. The roche pill would fizz in the quart of malt liquor until they were powder in your drink. This gave me an extra high. As I was doing this my dad said, "Hey give me some." I gave him one and he said, "Give me as many as you're taking." I explained how I already had a high tolerance and his response was, "Boy I was taking those types of pills since you were in diapers."

So I threw three roche pills into his quart, which was way less than I had taken. Traffic was bad. If you've ever been to California, you know the type of traffic I'm talking about. The roches started hitting my dad hard. He kept dropping his quart all over the floor of the car and I kept telling him, "Hey, you're wasting your quart and the roches." He was so messed up he ended up crashing into a car in front of us.

I remember thinking, "Man! I came all the way to California just to get busted the first day." It wasn't hard to smell the alcohol since my dad had dropped the quart of malt liquor so many times, not to mention that when he crashed, he dropped his quart and it flew all over the place. Before he crashed I tried to wake him up. He was totally knocked out in the driver's seat of the vehicle. I yelled at him, saying, "Hey, wake up! You're gonna crash!" and BAM, he hit the car in front of us.

An Asian guy came out yelling. Dad woke up when we crashed, and tried to hide the drugs and alcohol before the cops got there. My dad started yelling at this guy too. He got out of the car and they were yelling at each other. I was in the vehicle trying to clean up my dad's mess. His quart of malt liquor was by the gas pedal, almost empty. We were in traffic so we couldn't just flee the scene. I put the drugs up as best I could and put the quarts of alcohol all the way in the back of the vehicle, covered with clothes that were in there.

The cops came to the scene, and I watched as my dad, all pilled out, yelling back and forth with the cop and the Asian guy. I couldn't believe it. I was thinking I was busted for sure. To my amazement the cop never even came over to the vehicle. This blew my mind considering the situation. My dad got back into the vehicle and said, "Yeah, I was telling the cop that the guy would go, then break, then go and I hit him by accident." Both vehicles were still in working condition. Since we were in traffic I guess they gave each other their information and the cop told them both to leave. I couldn't believe my luck.

We got to his apartment. I've always heard the weed out in Cali was the bomb - grade A stuff, so I ended up walking around the corner. I stood by this car and some gang members rolled up saying, "What's up?" and I said, "What's up?" back. I asked them if they would sell me some weed. They looked at me and said, "You're not from around here, are you? We don't recognize you." I said, "No, I'm from Chuco town," which is the nickname for El Paso. They call El Paso that because Pachucos, which were old school Mexican gangsters, actually originated from El Paso. In my mind, everyone knew who Chuco town was, but they didn't. They said, "What's that, homie?" I said, "El Paso, Texas". They didn't even know about El Paso.

"I'm from Texas."

"Orale, are you a Sureño or Norteño?"

"Neither, there's no such thing as colors in El Paso. We just gang bang."

Now in California this is a big thing, and the only reason I even knew what they were talking about is because of a guy that used to go to high school with me in El Paso. He was from California. He used to buy drugs from me and had explained everything to me. If you were a Surño, which was Southern California, you would rock and represent the color blue. On the flip side, if you were from Northern California you were a Norteño and would rock and represent the color red. Out there, this was a big thing. A lot of people would die over this.

"You don't look like a rat. Yeah, we will sell you some weed, and come back to pick you up so we can party, homie."

"Alright."

"Hey homie, keep a look out real quick. Let us know if you see anyone."

"OK." The next thing I knew, these guys busted the window in a car, got in and hot-wired it.

As they were leaving in the stolen car they said, "Hey, homie, we will be back to pick you up to go party with us in like fifteen minutes.

"I'll be here." This is when I met the LC14 gang.

When they finally came back for me they had the weed, and in El Paso even if you just bought a $20 bag you could roll like 30 to 40 joints. I bought a $20 bag of California weed from these guys, and the $20 baggie they gave me was so small. You were lucky to roll three piners out of it which would be three real skinny joints. I got mad.

"Hey, you Vatos, think I'm stupid? You're trying to rip me off. I sell weed and this ain't no 20." I think these guys tripped out on how bold I was.

"You must get a lot for $20 in Texas, huh."

"Yeah."

They laughed. "We will hook you up homie. Get in the car. Let's go party."

I got in and they handed me a dime size bag like I would get in El Paso. I was content, and they started to explain the drug trade in Cali, and explained what they gave me actually is a 20 in California. They asked if the weed was any good in El Paso, and I explained how there was some "bunk" weed, which meant no good, but that I always got "bomb" weed, which was really good. This California weed was out of this world. They called it "indough" and this weed actually had crystals on it with all types of different colors like purple, orange, and red. It was crazy- and potent. California weed was so sticky it would actually stick to your fingers and you had to cut it with scissors to put it in the paper to roll a joint. When I smoked it I was high as a kite. I had never experienced weed like this in Texas. The weed was so gooey that the paper you used to roll the joint would even look kind of wet. It was crazy. One little joint of this California weed would equal the equivalent of maybe 30 El Paso joints put together, and maybe still stronger and more potent. So my new friends told me they would hook me up with good size bags whenever I wanted, since they grew it themselves and sold it.

We were cruising, and they asked what I drink, meaning what kind of alcohol, and I told them.

"You in Cali now, homie." To each other they said, "Let's go get this homeboy some 8 ball."

I found out what that was when we went to the liquor store.  The oldest homeboy of theirs was older than twenty-one so he could buy alcohol. He comes out with forty-ounce quarts of malt liquor named Old English 800 - that was 8 Ball. We started drinking it. I had not heard of, nor tried 8 Ball before, but I liked it, not because it tasted good, but because it was strong.

"We're Norteños. Our gang is LC14 which stands for Latino Crew 14." Their neighborhood looked no different from mine back in Jackie's. Their gang graffiti could be seen on all walls in their turf. I remember they broke some of their own rules by showing me where their turf started and ended.  Northern California street rules were that Mexicans not cross into the African American blocks where the blacks controlled stuff.  This was very different to me, because El Paso is pretty much a Mexican American city, a Chicano city. California was totally different, but just as crazy. Mexicans wouldn't go into the Black's territory and vise versa. It usually meant shoot-outs if either did so. Guns and shootouts are normal in California ghettos, from what I saw, and everyone was strapped, that is everyone had guns. Drive-bys and shootouts were a normal occurrence in California.

They were kind of showing me the ropes and I got along great with them. We lived the same type of lifestyle.  We even dressed the same; the only difference between El Paso gang bangers was that we didn't claim Thirteen or Fourteen. We would wear blue or red. It didn't matter to us. El Paso was all desert, and California was luscious and green with beautiful ocean and lakes everywhere.

I asked these new California homeboys if they like roches. They said yes immediately. I started hooking them all up. They would trip out because I would give them so freely. I didn't care. Life was a party, and I never knew when I was going to die so I was living it up to the fullest.

Later on, a homeboy from LC14 nicknamed Tejano (he'd been born in Texas, but grew up in California) tells me roches go for 10 to 15 dollars a pill in Califas.

"No wonder everyone's happy when I hook them up. I got them for 10 cents a pill in Mexico!" So I started selling them and trading them for drugs. Tejano and I became pretty close home boys. Everyone already knew me as Huero from Texas, and everyone showed me love and respect. They knew I was crazy and down just like them.

I would always be kicking it with them. It was a normal thing to see them throwing blows and fighting, just like we did in my neighborhood. Guys would always be walking around with black eyes from fighting with each other. I would throw blows too. It was exciting.

The Cali gangsters sold crack. Crack was nothing new to me, but that was the main drug I saw being sold. It made them a lot of money. In El Paso, heroine, roches, and cocaine were the main drugs sold. I remember seeing guys on bicycles on every corner there, and crack users they would call "crackheads."

I even used to sell fake crack and steal crackheads' money. When cops would cruise by, the guys would flee on their bicycles so they wouldn't get caught. Cops out there would beat you up if they caught you doing anything illegal. Again, this was nothing new. The cops in El Paso were the same way. My homeboys and I from Jackie's would get beat up all the time by cops.

Another thing they did at a whole other level in California was stealing cars. Man, they loved stealing cars. I must have witnessed them steal around ten cars. I have to admit I participated quite a few times. I actually learned how to break into and start stolen cars. You could tell these guys were pros at it and had been at it a long, long time. I also stole quarters out of the washers and dryers at my dad's apartment complex. I would break into them and get like 150 bucks. I remember cops being called out and talking to my dad and his wife. They later found out it was me because they found all the quarters in a bag I had in their apartment.

Dad wouldn't say too much, though, because he knew I was mad at him for leaving me when I was nine. I had confronted him multiple times, sometimes even wanting to throw blows and fight him.

He'd say, "I'm not gonna fight you, you're my son."

Around this time is when I first snorted a line of meth. I told the guys from LC14 to give me real big line and they asked if I'd ever done meth before.

"I've snorted cocaine."

"This ain't the same thing."

"Whatever, give me a big line." After I snorted this big line which must have been a 20 of meth, I thought man, they weren't lying! I stayed up for three straight days, amped out of my mind. I couldn't sleep or eat, and the top of the inside of my mouth felt numb. It was crazy, and after that you'd think I wouldn't do it again, but nope, not me. I started snorting meth and smoking it with weed rolled in joints on the regular for the two or three months I was in Cali.

A gang war started with LC14 and a rival gang, and I was smack down in the middle of it. The rival gang would come to LC's turf and we would throw blows with them. People were starting to get stabbed and shot. At this point I had been there several months. During the last two weeks I was in Cali, that rival gang ended up going to LC14's territory. Enemy gang members pulled up with guns, got out of their car and started shooting one of the guys from LC14 I had gotten to know pretty well. He didn't care when they started shooting. He started running straight towards them and got shot in his head and died. This really took everything to a whole new level. I wasn't there the day he got killed. I was partying at a lake with some of the guys from LC14, but they started retaliating. I went to the enemy gang's territory with the guys from LC14, and I actually put a guy in the hospital from beating him with a hammer. The guy lived, but the violence was escalating and getting out of control. But again, this was the life I lived and I was down for the cause, as they would say in the streets.

I would be returning to El Paso very soon, because I found out something had happened to my little sister.

18.

## Revenge Rampage

I was partying with one of my dad's neighbors, and as we drank and smoked weed, she let it slip that something bad had happened to my little sister back in El Paso. I wasn't expecting to hear this, and I was infuriated and wanted to go back immediately. I was shaking with anger. I wanted to kill the guys who had messed with her, and to make matters worse, I found out it was a gang that was scared of me. They didn't know it was my sister who they'd messed with.

When I got some money together, and with Grandma Racheal's help, I was on a plane back to El Paso. When I got there I went on a rampage - beating and stabbing guys from this gang who had hurt my little sister. I was on the hunt for that gang, their friends, and any family of theirs.

My homeboys from Jackie's found out and were on the warpath right along with me. I returned to my drug dealing and living the same way I did before I left.

One thing I noticed when I got back to Jackie's was a lot of the homeboys were locked up, doing multiple years' time. Everyone was building their rap sheet and their record, and everyone was starting to get months to years. Now some of my homeboys would never get out, since we were 100 percent hardened criminals who had our wrap down.

I was in the east side cruising around with some of my east side homies, high as a kite, on acid, smoking weed, and bumping the bass as usual. We were passing the high school I used to attend when lo and behold; I saw some of the guys from the gang who had wronged my sister, along with some of their friends and family members. I told my east side homeboys to stop the ride.

I got out.

"What's up?"

"What's up, Huero?" They knew me. You could see the sheer terror in their eyes. "You guys are from so and so gang aren't you?"

"You know this girl," and gave my little sisters name, "you guys messed with the wrong girl. That's my baby sister." I pulled my screwdriver out. These guys started running.

I was high on acid and that particular day and was so messed up I felt like I was Superman on steroids. I caught up to them fairly quickly, and I started stabbing as many of them as I could. They were freaking out, yelling, even crying. They tried to fight back.

Me, and the homies in the car with me, totaled around three or four guys against around seven of them, but I didn't care. I was so mad and had so much rage that it didn't matter. I was going to show them what was up when they mess with my loved ones. One of the guys I was attacking actually kicked me between my legs as hard as he could while I was stabbing his friend. I remember turning around and laughing. I was so messed up on acid I felt no pain.

I turned my wrath towards him, stabbing him. After a while, my homeboys said, "Hey Huero, let's go. Cops are gonna come."

One of the guys I was with told me years later that he really tripped out when all that happened, because in his mind, when I told him to stop the car he thought, "I'm down to throw blows with these guys and get down, even if we were outnumbered," but what he didn't expect was for me to trip out so bad and start stabbing everyone.

"Bro, you looked demonic. I can still picture you getting into my ride with you holding the bloody screwdriver right in front of your face, with blood all over you."

This happened right as school got out. I guess they were walking home from school when the incident occurred. We hid the screwdriver, and then I went home to Grandma Rosemary's mobile home. I got something to eat, and I remember telling her what happened.

"I just stabbed three or four guys a little while ago."

"Isaiah, don't be playing like that."

I wasn't playing. I was eating a bologna sandwich.

Hurting or stabbing people really didn't bother me. I liked the rush, the power.

I went outside because some guys had stopped by to buy some weed and roches from me. I was doing the drug deal in front of my grandma's house, counting the pills out and getting the weed ready to hand them. This low-rider passed by real slow. Twice it passed by, then a third time. I started yelling at the car, saying, "What's up? Where you from?" but I couldn't see anyone because the car had tinted windows.

I took the money and handed the guys their drugs.

The car came back again, this time stopping right in front of us. I was getting ready to throw down with them. I thought it was gang members in the car. As soon as it stopped right in front of us, around ten cop cars with lights flashing pulled up into the front of my grandma's house. I threw the roche pills everywhere and scattered the weed on the dirt and covered it with my shoes as fast as I could. The guys in the low-rider with tinted windows were undercover cops.

The cops didn't find me for drugs. They were there because of the guys I had just stabbed. They came out of their cars with guns drawn.

"Are you Isaiah Blancas?"

"I am."

They started beating me up, punching me in my ribs, cussing at me and saying, "You like stabbing people, huh?" They rushed into my grandma's house with their guns drawn, looking for the screwdriver.

My uncle told me later on that he was laying on his bed smoking a cigarette and  sharpening a real big Bowie knife, like 15 inches long, when the cops kicked his door in and said, "Freeze!" I could just imagine the cop's faces. It cracked me up for a long time, because I could just imagine him holding his big knife in the air with a cigarette in his mouth. I could also picture the cops looking for evidence and seeing my uncle, who is probably around 6'4" and husky, with a big old knife. It was funny to me.

"Isaiah, what did you do this time?" I'll never forget the look on Grandma Rosemary's face.

I was a horrible kid. Man, I can't even imagine how my grandma felt, taking care of a delinquent kid like me. She was always trying to preach to me about God. The truth is at that time in my life I didn't consider how anyone else felt around me.

I didn't even care about myself.

19.

Trapped by the Ankle

I was sent back to the detention home and this time for serious charges. They charged me with assault with a deadly weapon, which was a 1st degree felony. They dropped attempted murder charges which would have been worse.

There I was, rolling in the back of a cop car, handcuffed. I'd gotten accustomed to this and also accustomed to going into the detention home. I remember going through a gate. The cops would have to speak into a speaker. Then barbed wire gate would open and they would take you through a backdoor into the detention home. I guess it was the intake. Then they put you in a holding cell with one chair in it until a guard came. They checked to see if you had any contraband. This meant getting butt naked, and then the guard would ask your clothing size and give you inmate clothing - blue shorts, blue van shoes with no laces, and a white shirt and a blue shirt to wear on top of your white shirt. Off to the dorms you would go where you were going to be spending your time.

There was an employee there named Beto who everyone knew. He was an alright guy, famous for walking into the dorms early when it was time for you to wake up.

"Good morning, homeboys!"

A lot of guys who tried to act tough on the outside world, would say, "Yeah, we were in the D home, too."

One quick way you could find out if they were lying was to ask if they knew Beto and ask about his favorite saying. If they didn't know it, they were lying, and you knew they were fakes.

I had to go to court shackled up, cuffs on my ankles with a chain going up to my waist, with cuffs around my hands and a chain that would wrap around the waist chained to your cuffs. The court system for juveniles was in the detention home itself.

My grandparents were there waiting for me. This is the first time I found out why I had gotten busted so fast. The guys I stabbed were in the courtroom. I found out they had given law enforcement my nickname and real name. They had ratted on me, which was a violation of the street code. I was furious.

One of the guy's big brothers from their gang was there, and he was mad dogging me. I mad dogged him right back. He started throwing gang signs at me and I started throwing my gang signs right back at him.

"Isaiah, stop it!" Grandma Rosemary was always trying to correct me.

The judge was furious. "Mr. Blancas, if you don't stop, I'm going to give you years behind bars."

I was looking at some time.

Back in my dorm, I was worked out; doing pushups and things of that sort, trying to release some anger at these guys ratting on me. I promised myself if I ever saw those guys or their stupid older brother on the streets again when I got out, "I'm gonna finish what I started."

There were certain things you could do at the D home to pass your time. Some would draw, work out, read books, or play handball. When your dorm was able to go to the gym, it was common to see my home boys from Jackie's there, or to hear that they had just gotten out.    There was also visitation. This made me angry because I would see a lot of the other guys visiting with their parents. My mom and dad were long gone and had been for years. I never received even a letter from either of them, but Grandma Rosemary would always be there and I was grateful for that.

On her first visit, she told me about this Jesus character again, and told me I had to stop getting into trouble.  It's not really what I wanted to hear, but I was still thankful she would visit me.

After some time in the detention home and going to a few court dates, my lawyer worked out a deal. I would get to go home on intense supervision, which meant I had to wear an ankle monitor. I couldn't leave my grandma's house. That ankle monitor would stay on for one year, according to the court system requirements. That's beside the intense probation I would be on until I hit the legal age of eighteen. Drug testing on a weekly basis would also be required. Regular home visits and phone calls from my probation officer, as well as community service hours were required, too.

I was set free. It felt good.

When I got out, a lot of my homeboys came to see me and wanted to get me high. I told them that I needed a certain pill they sold in Juárez, Mexico. There was nothing more that I wanted than to start getting high again and go back to my normal lifestyle, but I had to be smart about it.

My homeboys agreed. The pills I'm talking about would clean your system, no matter what kind of drugs you were dirty on. They were little white pills. You just take one a few hours before you were drug tested. Perfect. The detention home where I had to go to get drug tested would let you know a few hours early. You just had to drink a gallon of water quick, and then you would go use the restroom. When your urine turned clear, you were clean and ready for your drug test. So my homeboys went to Mexico to get me boxes of it. It was a well-known pill on the streets to pass drug tests. All the hard core criminals knew about it.

About a week later, they brought these magical pills to me, and there I was smoking my weed and doing my drugs again. Every week when I took the drug test, I came out clean as a whistle.

I wasn't used to being stuck at home so I would exercise a lot. It was better than being at the detention home. My probation officer called to check up on me often, and when she did, it was a crazy thing. She asked how I was doing and really wanted to help me get my life right. A lot of times, people living the lifestyle I lived, consider probation officers their enemy. Looking back at it, they were just doing their job, and some of them really wanted to see you do better in life.

The weeks were going by slow. Man, when you're locked up it's different, because in there it's a different world. People who lived like me understand what I'm saying, but being free on a monitor stinks. Man, I hated it. I wanted to go outside the house, even if just going to the store.

My cousin Izzy came to visit and he said, "Hey, let's go to the corner store and get some beer."

I told him, "I can't man. I'm on house arrest"

Even he told me, "Man, you got to start behaving better. Look at where this is getting you."

You know the old saying. It goes in one ear, then out the other. That's how it was with anyone telling me stuff like that. The truth is when you live a lifestyle like that it becomes addicting and it's kind of hard to explain it to the normal person. It's a rush. But man, how right they were and how wrong I was for not listening.

Grandma must have figured it the perfect time to have preachers come and talk to me. She knew guys that had lived just like me, who went through the system and prison system too, but now they loved God. They were preaching the gospel and trying to convert people to this Jesus character. Guys would come over and start telling me how bad they were and how Jesus saved their lives.

I especially remember one particular guy named Pepe. It was obvious he knew the streets and the system. He had spent years and years behind bars. He would tell me it's not the life I wanted, but again I wasn't listening. I wasn't trying to hear it, I hated hearing it. I wished they would all just shut up and let me live my life.

Besides this, and to make matters worse, they sent me to do my community service hours at a Victory Outreach Church in northeast El Paso where a whole bunch of gang members had changed and started living for this Jesus guy.

I met a guy there named Rudy. He was one of the head guys there, and had been from the LfL gang, the fatherless gang that my homeboy Tiny was from. Tiny was the home boy that did some of my tattoos. Rudy actually knew Tiny's dad, who was nicknamed Tiny, too.

Big Tiny had actually jumped Rudy into the fatherless gang. Rudy and I got along because I was able to connect to him on some gang stuff. He knew what I was there for.

"Hey, Huero, you're a crazy little homie. Why don't you let me go to court with you so the judge can show you leniency."

"No way. I ain't no punk. I meant to do what I did. I don't need your presence at my next court hearing."

We would go around the neighborhoods cleaning spray paint. We were supposed to be painting over the spray paint graffiti with five gallons of paint with rollers. I, on the other hand, would use the paint bucket and rollers to paint graffiti. I rolled PvJ WSL all over the walls.

I had been on house arrest now maybe a month to a month and a half. The courts started making me go to school full time. I was excited about this. I thought I was going to be able to go back to my high school again and start up my drug dealing there, and hustle some money, too.

But no, that didn't happen. They sent me to a school named Cesar Chavez, a school for people just like me, guys who were on probation, or had just gotten out of the detention home. There were a few guys who went there who actually had already been to adult prison. A lot of guys had a monitor bracelet on their ankle as well. I had to go to find out all the rules and the dress attire. I hated it. I was going to have to wear slacks with regular shoes and a white shirt with a tie. It was horrible.

Everything was really controlled there. The thing that stood out most in my mind was wearing a tie. I thought that was for goody two shoes. In my mind, people who wore ties grew up with a silver spoon in their mouth. I couldn't have been further from that. I was a gangster, not a dumb nerd.

After a few months of this I had had enough. It was time to find some loopholes with the system.

20.

Escape Plan

I tried multiple things, but what ended up working was the night I turned off the electricity from my grandma's mobile home at the breaker box. I stayed home the next day. My parole officer called because when the power was off, the monitor would turn off because it was connected to the electricity. We assured her I had been at home. I started doing this every three days, during late nights. I would stay home just in case my parole officer or the cops would come to my house. After a few weeks of doing this, it didn't seem out of the ordinary anymore. My parole officer thought I was home. After feeling comfortable I could get away with it, I made my move.

First I started going right across the street to my homeboy's house where drug use and drug dealing were going on nonstop. I would party and sell drugs from there. I would only go out once every three nights, so it wouldn't be obvious. It worked. I made sure to get home by 4:00 a.m. every time. Once I felt 100 percent confident I wouldn't get caught going out, I started going multiple places around town. I started selling drugs with Juan again.

One time I had pounds and pounds of weed under my grandma's trailer.

"Isaiah, what are you doing?"

"Nothing, Grandma, why?"

"God gave me a dream last night, and he showed me an anaconda snake under my trailer, squeezing the life out of this house."

Really weird. It tripped me out so much we moved our drugs somewhere else.

One time I was growing marijuana plants in my grandma's backyard, and she tore them out of the ground and threw them away. Growing any type of plants in the desert is hard to do.

"Grandma, did you tear out my plants and throw them away?"

"Yes."

"Why?!" It made me mad.

"Because they're illegal."

I tried to lie, saying, "You got it all wrong."

"OK, what kind of plant was it?"

"It's an apricot plant."

"Apricots grow on trees."

I then shut up as my grandma gave me an earful. She would throw my drugs away if she found them, so I had to hide them really well.

Another time she threw like 150 roche pills away. We went through the same stupid question/answer deal.

"Grandma, did you throw my pills away?"

"Yes."

"Why? I need those pills."

"What are they?"

"My aspirins. I get bad headaches. I need them."

"Isaiah, they said roche right on back of the pill."

Again I shut up and got an earful from my Grandma Rosemary. You know now that I'm older and have kids of my own, I think of those days and how ignorant I was. I see right through my own kids when they're trying to run game by me, just like my grandma did me.

One late night when I sneaked out across the street, I was all roched up. I was doing the all same things again when I could. Juan and I were talking outside. I was standing, he was in his car getting ready to leave and he pulls a gun out. He always had guns on him. He said, "I'm gonna shoot a bullet right between your shoes." I was so messed up I said, "Go for it." The next thing I know he shot what must have been a 25 handgun, because the shot wasn't loud. Dirt flew as he shot between my shoes on the ground and I started laughing.

"You're crazy, Pee Wee. I'll be back in a few nights to steal some cars with you," he said.

"OK."

Three nights later we stole a vehicle that actually had a system in it. I remember we were cruising all pilled out, going to homeboy's houses in the east side, bumping the music. We went to Index's house and he was tripping out, saying, "Man, you're crazy."

My life started spiraling out of control again and I was ready to cut this monitor thing off my ankle. It was always on my mind. I was sick of playing by the rules, so one day my ex-girlfriend's cousin, whose nickname was Gizmo, called me.  He was on house arrest too. He lived a similar lifestyle to mine and I would sell him drugs. We partied together a lot. He was from east side of El Paso in an area nicknamed Polvos. We started talking and he tells me he's sick of being on house arrest. I told him I was too. So we planned to cut our ankle bracelets at the same time and go on the run. The next day we talked on the phone and said, "Let's do this."

We both cut our bracelets and then met up not too far from where he lived. We were walking through the desert, discussing and planning our next move, when we see a guy walking towards us in the middle of the desert. Gizmo and I had stolen some quarts of alcohol before walking through the desert. I figured I'd rob this guy. We needed money.

"Que rollo?" I said, which means 'what's up?'

The guy said 'What's up?' back.

I said, "Give me your feria, homes," which means 'give me your money.'

I could see this guy was really scared.

"I don't have none."

I threw my quart of beer as hard as I could at his head but I missed. It whizzed right by his head and Gizmo said, "What are you doing? We're going to get busted."

I was in a zone in my mind, and I thought, "I'm taking what he has whether he likes it or not."

The guy started running, and I was right behind him. Now check this out. There was one two-story house in the middle of the desert where we were. This guy ran inside it. Come to find out it was his house. Just my luck. Eight to ten guys came out with bricks in hand and start beating the crap out of me.

 Gizmo ran away. I only saw him because one of the bricks they threw hit me in the head. While on the hot desert ground, I saw him. When he saw they were beating me up, he ran back to help me. The guys beating me up had called the cops, and they arrived pretty quickly. There we were, handcuffed behind a cop car headed to their headquarters. I remember

Gizmo saying we hadn't even been on the run but a few hours. I told him to be quiet. I was mad that we had gotten caught so quickly. Our plan fell apart because I had to rob someone.

At the station, the cops sat us down handcuffed to chairs where their computers and monitors were. I started spitting all over their computers. Gizmo kept telling me to stop because the cops were going to beat us up. At this point I didn't care. Our warrants were supposed to pop up on their computer system immediately, since we were on house arrest, and Gizmo's did.

Mine didn't, and as the guys had beaten me up so badly, they were not pressing charges. They let me go. I couldn't believe my luck.

Later on, Gizmo told me they made him clean all my spit off the computers, and had roughed him up some. I laughed. He said it was messed up because I was the one trying to pull a robbery and he got locked up and I didn't.

I had to get out of El Paso for a little while, until things cooled down, but before I left town I planned to have some fun. Since I had been on intense probation and the monitor, I felt it was time to let loose. I went to get my stuff from my grandma's.

On my way there I got stabbed in the stomach. Now I had cut myself when I was younger and burnt cigarettes on my arm, but never had I been stabbed. I'm not going to give information on this subject, but it was a crazy situation.

I was all messed up on roche pills and alcohol. Flesh was hanging out from my stomach, and it looked like a bunch of little bubbles where the two pieces of my stomach had split in two from the stab wound. Blood squirted from my stomach.

I went to my grandma's and pushed my flesh back in. My uncle sewed me up pretty good, and then he put a cloth patch around my wound. He washed it with alcohol then dried it, and then put a piece of gauze with tape around my stab wound.

I kept partying and never went to the hospital. For the next week I tried not to walk as much, because every time I had too much movement, my stab wound would open back up and bleed. I had to change the gauze every day for three or four weeks until it finally scabbed up.

This kind of made me chill out even if I didn't want to. I also wasn't staying anywhere near my grandma's house. I was in the west side at the Jackie's projects, staying with homeboys. I knew the cops would be looking for me at Grandma's.

Around this time a lot of the homeboys and homegirls were on a corner end of the Jackie's projects. There must have been forty to fifty of us. They all knew what had happened to me and how I had gotten stabbed. I still had gauze and tape on my stomach. I was still healing from the wound. My homeboys would trip out on me, telling me I was crazy. A few guys from the east side gang I didn't get along with were walking by. I didn't know what gang they were from until my homeboys told me. My friends knew I didn't like them, and they told me they hadn't started problems with the rival gang yet because they wanted to hit them up with me. So they gave them a pass to walk by, but not through the Jackie's projects. They were waiting until I got there as kind of a surprise for me.

I didn't believe them, so I yelled, "Hey, where you vatos from?" and they said, "The east side," and claimed the gang I hated. I got mad and started charging toward them.

My homeboys said, "Hey, Huero, we will beat them up. You're still healing from your stab wound."

"I'll hit them up by myself." So I did. I was trying to throw blows with them. They were scared. They'd already heard of me.

There were three of them and a girl. The girl got between us and was pleading for them. They were big time scared, and my gang was there with me.

I heard, "Hey, Huero, que rollo, con estos vatos?" The person asking me this was an old-school homeboy that had just arrived and had just been released from prison. He didn't even give me a chance to beat them up. He started wailing on them, beating all three of them at a whole different level. When they were on the ground, bleeding from the beating they had just received, the girl was yelling at them to get up and run.

All my homeboys were laughing at them, and my old school homie went to get a gun from his vehicle and started shooting at them. He was all amped up and yelling, "That's what's up with the Jackie's gang!"

This was a normal occurrence where I grew up. When one of us from Jackie's would be stabbed or shot, it was normal for our gang to retaliate. There are countless stories I can tell about that.

I stayed on the run a few months in El Paso. I was also crossing pills again from Juarez, Mexico. One of the times I got arrested for the roches, but not on the American side, on the Mexico side. I even ended up going to jail in Mexico. You won't believe what they wanted for me to get out of jail. They wanted a bucket of chicken from the American side. So my homeboys brought them a bucket of chicken and they let me out. I wished the U.S. would release me for buckets of chicken. It cracked me up.

After this I fled to California and went back to the LC14 neighborhood.

When I got there I saw Tejano, and he said, "What's up, Huero? You back in Califas, huh?"

I said, "Yeah, I'm on the run." I noticed a lot of the vatos weren't there anymore. I asked Tejano, "Where's your homeboys at?" He told me a lot of them had died or were locked up. He then told me him and another older homeboy of his were on the way to L.A., Southern California, to start a new life.

I said, "You gonna run into a whole bunch of enemies out there, ain't you??

He said, "Naw, we already got some homeboys that are Norteños out there, but it's all good. It is what it is."

That's the last time I saw Tejano.

I stayed in Cali for a few months, and then headed back to El Paso. I was sixteen-years- old by this time. I had been stabbed and shot at multiple times, and I was doing the same things I always did. Back at my grandma's, everything had cooled down with the law, but I still stayed at Jackie's a lot, too.

One time when I went to Jackie's, we started partying with a guy named Tito who had moved to the projects from the northeast side of town. He knew my uncles and cousins. He sold drugs too, so we started partying in the west side, and then we ended up in the northeast at a party packed with a gang that was from there. This was their turf and they were pretty well known themselves, so it was me, my homeboys Cruz and Barney. We were the only three there from the west side.

I had a white shirt on I'd bought downtown at a store named La Negrita that was known to all El Paso gang members. Everyone in gangs shopped there for gangster clothing. I bought white shirts there sometimes. La Negrita store had old English letters that could be ironed on your shirts, and on my brand new white shirt I had them iron old English letters that spelled out West Side Locos real big.

When we walked into this northeast party and Tito was looking for one of his homeboys located all the way in the back of the party. We went through many rooms until he found him. I remember oldies blasting from their stereo system and barrels of beer everywhere and there must have been around fifty gang members up in there.

When we finally found Tito's homeboy, he looked at us and my shirt with the big West Side Locos logo on it.

"Hey, homie, this is our turf. Can you take that shirt off out of respect? We don't have no problems with your gang, but this is our turf, not yours."

As I always carried a knife or screwdriver on me, I was already thinking, "I'm going to stab as many of them as I can." I was looking around and we were cornered in at the back of the party. There was nowhere to go and Barney looked at me all paranoid. He knew I wasn't going to do it.

"I'm not taking my shirt off."

Then Barney started telling me, "Hey Huero, this ain't our turf, and they're even asking you. They aren't looking for problems."

"I ain't doing it."

My friend Cruz, years later, said, "I knew you weren't gonna take your shirt off, so I was getting ready to throw down."

As I was talking to my homeboys, Tito started talking to his homeboy, the one telling me to take my shirt off. He changed almost immediately. He said, "Hey, are your uncles so and so?" and I said, "Yeah." He then said, "Keep your shirt on, homie," as he pumped the barrel of beer and handed me a cup. He said, "Tell your uncles I say 'Hi."

As I said before, my uncles were much respected in the streets. I later found out one of my uncles stuck a big knife in a guy's necks just for knocking on my aunt's door looking for my cousin. I think my uncle thought he was my cousin's enemy, but he was actually a friend of my cousin's. My cousin said they never knocked on her door again.

I had been on the run going on a year, but my luck and life on the run was going to end soon.

I had gotten my girlfriend pregnant.

21.

I'm a Dad

You'd think this would change my view on life, but it didn't. I did say, though, that I would be there for my kid. I didn't want my child feeling like I felt not having a dad around, but I was lost in the lifestyle I was living. I could be dead soon, or locked up for a long time.

My life kept going downhill.

Back in Jackie's, many of my homeboys were starting to get locked up more often. The cops started to crack down on our gang. We started seeing cops a lot more. It was nothing new to have them messing with us, or beating us up. I remember Indio would always throw rocks at the cop cars or flip them off.

One cop in particular always tried to bust him. They pulled up on us and Indio threw a rock at him and flipped him off. We all ran into the desert. They just wanted to catch Indio and this time they finally did. They gave him the beating of a lifetime and took him to jail. We didn't see him for a few weeks. When he was released from jail, we all laughed as he told us about the beating he received.

Back on the east side, I started breaking into houses. I got the call my baby girl was going to be born. I showed up to the hospital high on weed and roches. I was messed up, so my girlfriend's mom was very angry and rightfully so. I held my daughter for the first time. I couldn't believe I was a dad.

It would be the last time I held her for a long while.

I left the hospital and I went back across the street from my grandma's house where I met up with some homeboys. The first thought in my head was that I needed to get some money to buy my newborn daughter some clothes and diapers. A guy there started telling me how he knew of a house where there was money, gold, and guns.

## 22.

## Real Jail

"Let's go rob it," I said.

"What, right now?" It was still day time.

"Right now."

He looked scared, like he didn't want to go.

"Get up and take me to this house right now. If you don't, I'm going to stab you."

He wasted no time, but took me to the house he'd been talking about a few blocks away. When we arrived we knocked on the door to make sure no one was home. When no one answered we went to the back of the home and checked if any windows were open. One was, so I made this guy jump through the window first, and then I followed. I looked for money, jewelry, and guns, stuff that was worth money.

The guy I was with said, "Hey, look at these video games."

I almost lost my mind. I got real mad and cussed at him. "Don't be stupid! Look for money, gold and guns, stuff of value." After getting what I wanted to get, I looked through their refrigerator to see what they had to eat and found a pizza box with some leftover pizza. I went out the front door eating a slice of pizza. I don't know if any neighbors saw me and called the cops, but as I was walking back to Grandma Rosemary's, the cops stopped me and asked what I was doing and where I was going.

I said, "I'm going to my grandma's which is a few blocks away, and I'm just enjoying my day eating a pizza." I tried to be as calm as I could, since I had roche pills hidden on me, and I had stuck one of the guns I had stolen, a shotgun, inside my pants through my waist area. It was hard trying to walk with it.

The cops said, "We're gonna pat you down real quick. If everything's cool, we will let you go on your way." They took the pizza box away from me and started searching me. They felt the shotgun immediately.

"Don't move, or were gonna shoot you," and pulled their guns out on me.

I was busted.

They found the shotgun along with three other guns I had stolen, and the gold. They even knew the exact address of the property I had stolen from. The pizza delivery box had the address right on it. I was handcuffed and put in back of the squad car. They didn't find the roche pills.

At the station, they discovered the warrant for cutting off my monitor and fleeing on probation. I knew I was going to do some time.

The cops laughed, saying, "What were you thinking, Bro? Robbing that house and eating their pizza, you must have been pretty hungry."

The pizza box and everything else I'd stolen was on a table for evidence. I usually cussed the cops and tried fighting them. I hated cops. They were my enemies. But I had to be pretty cool this time because of the roche pills I had hidden on my body. I asked them if I could use the restroom and they agreed. They took me to their restroom, took off my handcuffs and closed the door. They waited outside the bathroom door and said, "Let us know when you're done so we can cuff you back up."

This was my chance to take out my roche pills and eat them. I usually took tons of roches a day, but I would take a certain amount. I just kept popping pills all day and all night long. I had a bag with maybe 20 to 25 roches inside and I stuck the whole bag in my mouth. I chewed the pills along with the bag. I didn't want them having any more evidence on me. It was a miracle they didn't find them to begin with. I think they figured they had busted me with so much evidence that I couldn't possibly have anything else on me.

They handcuffed me again and put me back into the holding cell. The pills kicked in fast. I didn't wake up until the next morning.

They sent me back to the detention home. I went to court and they decided to try me as an adult, since my seventeenth birthday was right around the corner. The El Paso County Jail accepted you as an adult if you were seventeen, so I went to a few more court dates which took months.

I was to be transferred as an adult to the El Paso County Jail. I'd heard many stories at the detention home about adult jail and how bad it was. I found myself shackled up, going straight there to find out how true those stories were.

As I entered, I went up an elevator where the holding tanks were. When the guards put you in the elevator they say, "Face towards the back of the elevator. No turning around or looking our way." This was in the mid-1990s when all the prison gang/mafias were at war in the Texas prison system. There was no babying you.

I remember one guy ignoring what the guards told him. He turned around and faced the guards to ask a question. They beat this guy hard core. When the elevator opened, they were cussing at us, saying, "You don't want to listen? We're gonna beat you too."

I could see I was no longer at the detention home. This was a very serious place compared to the juvenile system, and these guards weren't there to sympathize or talk or be your friend. I understood quickly they considered people like me their enemy. I thought, "I'm going to have to be even more hardcore here." I had not even made it to the holding tanks yet.

When I got there, I was in the holding tank for like ten to fifteen hours before they called me out. I had never been there before. As they opened the steel door, I just stepped outside of it, waiting for instructions. A guard then yelled at me, cussing, saying, "Hey, get over here!" So I went. They asked if I had any tattoos, which gang I belonged to, and then sent me to an area down the hall for fingerprints. Then they said I could use the phones if I wanted to call someone.

I didn't have a bond, so I called my grandma and talked to her for a bit until the guards said, "That's it, get back into the holding tanks." Then the next guy came out to start his booking process. Now this kind of tripped me out because at the detention home you were not allowed phone calls except once or twice a month with adult supervision. But at adult jail it was different. The holding cell held around fifty guys. You could barely walk through the room and it smelled bad, like feet and alcohol, or guys that hadn't showered.

After a few hours, they called my last name. In adult jail or prison systems they call you by either your last name or inmate number. My last name was called along with countless others. We went to another holding tank on the other side of the jail. There were many holding tanks so when I entered this one, I saw two guys I knew from the streets, and one guy I was locked up with at the detention home years ago.

He said, "Hey, you're Huero from Jackie's, huh?"

An older guy, twice my age from our biggest rival gang in the west side said, "That's where you're from?"

"Yeah."

"If we end up in the same tank upstairs, you already know what it is."

I said, "I know what it is, and we don't have to wait until we're upstairs. We could get down now."

This guy was twice my size but I didn't care. I wasn't going to show any weakness. After spending another ten to fifteen hours at this holding tank, it was time to go upstairs to start doing my time. First they took us to a room and told us to get butt naked. They were checking us for contraband and anything illegal.

They gave you different colored clothing depending on your charges.  For instance, if you were in green you were there for tickets and wouldn't be there long. Blue meant you had a federal case, and if you were in orange, the color I was given, you were considered the worst. You were either a violent offender or had felony court cases pending. The green beans and the guys in blue had the option to work in the kitchen or clean the facility. The guys in orange like me were not able to.

After this you would be given a shower, naked, in front of everyone. They would squirt shampoo on your head that would kill lice or germs.

There were lockdown tanks, segregated tanks, for guys who were in prison gangs/mafias or inmates who would not listen or follow rules. Little did I know I would be spending months upon months there.

As I waited for my turn to shower, a guy in one of the cells said, "Hey, you're from Jackie's."

I said, "Yeah," and I asked him where he was from. He was from a rival gang in the west side but he said, "I'm into other stuff now." He meant a prison gang.

I said, "Orale wey." Back in that time, everyone used that as a slang word, kind of a bad word. It was kind of like, "What's up?"

We all talked that way once in a while.

He said, "Ese homes, don't call me that wey, por favor." He explained how that's pee wee slang and OGs don't like that word. I said, "Alright." He taught me it was considered disrespectful. So from that day on I never said that word again.

When you joined any prison gang/mafia, there were no longer fights between rival gangs. As a matter of fact, a lot of times your enemies would become your friends. You follow jail and prison rules. If you start riding with the same family prison gang, all that street stuff goes out the window. It's not tolerated.

After leaving the lockdown tanks and showering, I went to the first tank where I'd be spending time, but first I had to get my bed, which was as thin as a pillow and you had to carry it to your tank, folded in half. Inside your bed were the bed sheets, a blanket, and a towel to shower with. There was a little bag with a thin black hair comb, a small tube of toothpaste, a toothbrush, a little bar of soap, and a BIC razor.

So into the tank I went. The gated bars opened, I walked in, and then they closed. Everyone was looking at me. The head guy controlling the tank said, "Come to my room to go over the rules." Before he started giving me the tank rules, he said, "Where you from?"

I said, "PVJ WSL."

"Your homeboy Koko pulled out a shotgun on someone's girlfriend." He wasn't supposed to. It was a fellow gang member of his. "You guys have a green light on you because of it, but I'm gonna let that pass because we're at war with a lot of other prison gangs."

Then he then told me the rules. Cleaning was a big thing. It reminded me of my uncles. New guys had to clean the showers or toilets. I picked showers. Everyone had to get up to eat when food was given, and stand in line and get your food first, then walk back to get your drink. Everyone had to stand at the metal tables until a prayer was said over your food. Then you could sit and eat. There was no putting your hands over someone's food, or using the restroom when anyone was eating. The pay phone that was in the tank could only be used forty-five minutes by each inmate.

If anyone broke these rules there were consequences. The first time would be a warning and you would have to clean more. The second time you would have to lift your arms and a few guys would punch you in your ribs. The third time meant a ferocious beating, and after that there would probably be a stabbing.

He took me to the room where I'd be sleeping. After meeting everyone, I found out I was in a tank of almost all enemy gangs. Everyone there either didn't like or hated Jackie's. I kept to myself. I broke my BIC razor down to only the razor, just in case I had to fight multiple guys at once. I was in that tank for maybe three weeks until they moved me to another tank.

I talked to the head guy in charge, who was from a notorious, well-known gang. Everyone in El Paso knows this prison gang, as they controlled the jail and different prisons throughout Texas and the El Paso streets. This guy told me they were having some issues with the black inmates in the tank. There were a few Mexicans that were scared of the black guys in there. They were not street guys and were getting intimidated by these black inmates.

"There are three of us from the same prison gang in this tank, and we're going to make a move on the black inmates and the scared Mexicans when we go to sun porch." The sun porch was where you went to work out, play handball or just walk around feeling and seeing the sunshine. The sun porch was on the very top floor in the jail, and you were allowed to go out three times a week.

So then he asked if I was down to hit these vatos up with them. I said, "Yes." This is when I started getting involved with them. After the sun porch thing went down, we got locked down in the cells as soon as we got back. We weren't able to come out of our rooms and the tables turned. The black guys and these few Mexican guys were so scared after the incident they pushed the emergency button, which was a metal button on the wall of each cell. They told the guards on us and got shipped out to another tank. This prison gang controlled everything in there so it didn't matter which tank they would go to. They were going to have green lights on them and get real bad beat downs or get stabbed or killed.

This prison gang had members working in the kitchen, or as trustees who cleaned the whole jail and had access to everything. They even had certain guards on their payroll, so getting drugs in there or getting word throughout the jail or Texas prison system or even the streets was no problem. If they wanted to put a hit on you, you better watch your back. They were the real deal, nothing to be played with.

I started learning jail tactics from them. For instance, say that some marijuana was smuggled into the jail and we didn't have a lighter. So you would take three pencils, shave the wood off the pencil with a razor until only the lead remained. Two long pieces of lead would go into the electric socket, the third piece of lead would have toilet paper in the middle. You wrapped it with three to four inches of toilet paper so you didn't touch the lead that's exposed on both ends. You hold only the toilet paper, touch all three pieces of lead together and it lights like a lighter. I learned to reroute the pay phone wires in order to make free calls. Other inmates would pay collect call prices. These are a few things I learned from them.

After around a month a half, guards came and told me I was getting sent back to the detention home. I had one last court appointment to see how much time I was going to serve in the adult jail for breaking and fleeing from the juvenile system.

I was still wearing my orange colored felony clothes from the adult jail when I got back to the detention home. When they were taking me to the dorm, I saw my little homeboy Tiny. He was there in a boot camp program. We nodded at each other and he made a "J" with his hand. I did the same, representing our gang. I had to stay there around a week waiting for my court date.

I was seventeen so I went to a dorm with younger guys, but I was placed on lockdown. I can still remember to this day how different it was being at the detention home compared to adult jail. The detention home was such a safer environment.

They asked me how it was at the adult jail and I told them how crazy it was compared to where they were. I told them, "You better be ready to rumble there, if you don't change. There ain't no cookies and milk there before you go to sleep." They were used to having cookies and milk before sleep in the detention home.

When I finally got a date, the juvenile court system sentenced me to six months at the adult jail. This time I was going to the 2nd floor where inmates showered before going upstairs. It was called the rascal tanks. Everyone in those tanks was seventeen to twenty-one years old. It's where I would spend the rest of my time.

Earlier in the story you might remember that these were the lock down tanks. I went in and met everyone. A lot of the guys hadn't yet been sentenced. There was a guy there who was around my age, and he had been there two years already. He was fighting a murder charge. He told me they had offered him a life sentence, so he was fighting the charge. He actually hadn't killed anyone. His homeboys had picked him up after the murder and he had a spec of blood on his pants so small they had to actually use a microscope to detect it. They knew he didn't do it; all they wanted was for him to rat on his homeboys. They would drop all charges against him, but he wouldn't rat on them. He lived by the street code 100 percent.

They called the 2nd floor the "rascal tanks" because we were the rowdiest ones in the county. The older prison gang members went by rules, but a lot of us were crazy youngsters with a lot to prove. We would always be fighting, starting riots, or doing drugs. We were just wild in general.

After being there around two months, I was one of the guys running the rascal tanks. I was now the one giving rules when new inmates arrived.

## 23.

## Rascal Tanks

Now they didn't call these the rascal tanks for nothing. Our days and nights consisted of coming up with crazy things to do. There were many things, but I'll share with you a few.

We would make the newcomers fight whether they wanted to or not. We would have two guys, one on each side of the bars where the guards would come through occasionally to count the inmates. There were windows there, so you could see on both sides if guards were coming, and the inmates would alert us.

We would pick a cell and have one guy cover the emergency button, another four guys block the doorway so no one could go in or go out. We would make them fight until one or the other would knock the other out cold, or until one was real bloodied, or when they were too tired to continue. Then we would know who could throw blows and who was down, and who wasn't. Sometimes we would make them push the emergency button and ship themselves out to another tank if we felt they would end up ratting on us, or if we thought they weren't meant to be in our tank.

When you're locked up and bored, you come up with some crazy things to pass the time. We came up with another idea. So this one guy who was from Juarez, Mexico who was in our tank was being released. One time we saw him in his underwear. We all were laughing at him because his underwear was tight, and they were blue and had bleach spots on them. This guy was really short. We had him leave them when he was released. Instead of making new inmates fight, we gave them options. Option #1 was to get knocked out, but naked. Option #2 was dance in those little blue undershorts on a table, or option #3 was to fight in the room with another inmate, then get beat up by all of us really bad.

Believe it or not, most guys would dance with the underwear. It was hilarious to us. The TV in the tank had a channel that played music.

So we would put that channel on and make them dance. We all laughed so hard our stomachs hurt.

A lot of guys would choose the fighting and get beat up really bad.

We spent a lot of time locked down in our cells except to shower. We didn't care. It was worth the locking down for us to have some fun. I remember the whole county jail hearing what we were making inmates do in the rascal tanks. Food was delivered to our tanks three times a day. The inmates themselves brought the food with guards watching them to make sure no contraband was passed around. One guy from the dominant prison gang that controlled things (I had done time with him upstairs and he liked me) handed us our food.

"Hey, Huero, come here."

I said, "Yeah, que rollo."

"We heard what's going on here. We don't do the kind of stuff you're doing here. Get all the little homies on the ball. You're the one I'm gonna start speaking to on the tank's behalf."

I said, "OK, but it's just hearsay."

He laughed as if he knew I was lying. "Keep the homies in check."

"Alright, I will."

As he was leaving, he said, "I don't want to hear about this going on again."

I said, "OK," but we kept doing the same thing. Of course I wasn't going to tell him that, though afterwards I would see him and other guys when food was being delivered to our tank. I would be asked if everything was running smooth in our tank. I always said, "Yea, I'm on top of it." They were grooming me for the lifestyle. They gave me extra plates of food, sometimes up to ten extra plates. I would keep an extra and share the extras with the other inmates. Extra food was a big thing.

I saw my homeboy Indio giving food out a few times. He would always say, "What's up, Huero?" and I would say it back. He always gave me extra plates every time I saw him. One time he said, "I'm coming back with a few joints for you," and he did. I think it was two or three joints. We were high as a kite inside those rascal tanks that day. The big homeboys from the prison gang would send me drugs once in a while, too.

After a few months, Valdo and Cruz were in the rascal tanks on the same floor. I even sent Valdo a joint and some food to his tank from mine.

Later on he told me, "Man, the rascal tank you were in was loud. You could always hear noise coming from your tank." He remembered guards always coming to our tank to get control of things. We laughed about it.

I was there for eight months.

After my sentence was complete I did months at the detention home, months upstairs in the adult jail, and six months at the rascal tanks in the adult jail. Time served totaled around a year. So I was back on the streets. I was feeling tougher than ever, like I was untouchable and I was becoming what I aspired to be. Man, did I jump back into things at a whole new level.

I started into my old ways, but things were a whole lot more serious. Now I had an adult record, but to tell you the truth it didn't bother me at all. As a matter of fact it excited me.

I went to my grandma's house and visited with her. She was showing me my drawings on envelopes and handkerchiefs I'd made her from jail. She told how talented she thought I was, and how I could be an artist. I thought, "Yeah right, me an artist." I knew she was just trying to be positive about my situation.

After visiting my grandma, I went to Devin's to give him a Dickie jacket he had lent me. I actually got busted with it, so he waited all that time to get it back. We both laughed as we were smoking a joint, saying it still looked new. He had bought it only three days before I got busted so it was pretty much brand new in a bag in the county jail along with my other possessions. When you get locked up they zip lock your belongings until you're freed. It was funny to us then.

I went to go see my daughter. She was a lot bigger than when I held her for the first time when she was born.

As mentioned before, I was on my way to Jackie's to see my homeboys on the West side. When I got there I started partying with the homies. A lot of them were locked up and a lot of us were free, but that was normal to us all at that point in our lives. It just came with the lifestyle we had chosen to live. If we weren't locked up we were living the same way or worse than before we were locked up.

Around this time in my life I went to party one night with the home boys in Juarez, Mexico, and everyone was all messed up on alcohol and different drugs. I remember I saw some homies from the east side there partying too. A lot of them were on acid and one guy actually overdosed and died. I asked one of them, "Where did you guys buy your acid?" He told me the dealer's name, it was someone we mutually knew. The first thought that came to mind was, "I need to try it." Looking back at it, I was so lost and stupid. That's how I lived. I ended up trading some of this guy's killer acid for some weed. I remember taking like eight tabs, then I took two more because it wasn't hitting me. I was actually getting mad and I was gonna go beat him up really bad. I had traded him for fifty tabs. I took five more. I'd taken like fifteen tabs or more and all of a sudden they hit me. At first I was enjoying the high, then it got crazy and out of control. Someone I was with said, "Hey Huero, are you alright?" But what I heard was, "Hey, Huero, are you alright?" multiple times. Then I heard ringing in my ears and couldn't hear anyone. I started seeing dots, and everything went black. That's all I remembered. I found out clearly, as I woke up in the hospital that had overdosed and died. That didn't change anything or any choices I made, which were all bad at the time.

It was a common thing to see my homeboys from Jackie's shoot up and overdose and die. My homeboys knew how to do CPR, and they would bring them back to life themselves. Whoever had overdosed after receiving CPR would throw up white, then two homeboys would wrap their arms around them and then walk them around until they could walk themselves. It was as crazy as it sounds, but it was normal to us.

24.

## Pick Up and Delivery

I was out of control, and everyone I surrounded myself with, too. I started getting into alcohol at this time. I was always drinking and going to bars. It was crazy, because I almost never got asked for my ID. I guess they figured I was twenty-one or older. I got into fights. I went to some really ghetto bars, the kind where you had to be ready for someone to break a bottle on someone's head, and then stab them with the same bottle.

I liked those types of bars because I liked fighting. A homeboy of my uncles', named Suge, would see me at these different types of bars around town all the time. He asked me to start selling cocaine with him. He'd asked me years earlier. He would tell me, "You're a crazy little homie. You need to start riding with me on this cocaine thing. He'd seen me going in and out of jail and he knew I was down and he kept trying to recruit me. I always said no because I was already selling drugs.

I worked a construction job here and there. I had to because I was getting an apartment. I needed some type of legal income, but I still sold drugs and partied.

I liked working construction because it was like working out at the gym. Throughout my whole life, I always worked out. I had my apartment a few months until I ended up getting locked up again. This time I did three months for an assault, I think. To be honest, I don't remember why. I was always in trouble and in jail. Getting out changed nothing.

I ran into Suge. He asked me again.

"Hey, start rolling with me."

"Look, what do you want me to do?"

"Be a collector for me. If someone doesn't want to pay up, you deal with them however you have to get the money. It's up to you."

"How much will I get from this?"

"Half the profits."

"How much do people owe you?"

"It could be a thousand, could be twenty thousand. You'll also be selling cocaine with me."

It sounded amazing to me so I said, "Let's do it."

Suge had dealers at multiple bars where he did his collections, which is why I saw him in bars so often.

That's where I came in. Sometimes guys didn't want to pay, or they would get ripped off. We would find out who did it, and then I would go meet the guys and make sure they paid. Suge always had guns on him. He'd been doing this for years. He showed me a lot of new things in the criminal lifestyle. He'd been shot eight times with a gun once and lived. He'd been thrown out of a car going over 100 miles per hour and lived. They had beaten him so badly once that he could actually see his brain through his skull in a mirror before fainting, and lived. He was a career criminal, but I was too. That's all we knew. So we were always together.

I beat up guys badly to collect monies owed, or sometimes pulled a knife or a gun on them. They would usually get so scared at that point they would give the money right up. Some guys I knew preferred guns. I was more a knife type of guy.

I used to get asked, "Why do you like knives more than guns?"

"Because using a knife is up close and personal, and from my experience, a gunshot wound would leave a little hole, depending on the gun, but a knife leaves a big hole with blood squirting out." It just seemed more horrific to the person on the other end.

When we collected money at these bars, I would see a lot of homeboys I knew, and people I'd done time with. Sometimes I would run into the guys from the notorious prison gang I rolled with when I was locked up. I would always go say 'what's up' to them, no matter what I was doing as a sign of respect. I would kick it with them for a while.

When I wanted to stay at these ghetto bars too long, Suge would say, "Let's go party at some bars that are a little bit nicer." Now this is where I really learned to think and dream bigger than ever. It's crazy. You'd think you would learn from something or someone doing well in life, but I learned how to think big as a criminal. We started going to nice bars where people were just getting drunk and having a good time. That seemed out of this world to me. I was used to crazy places and parties where people would get stabbed or shot, or where you had to be on guard - places where you already knew something crazy was going to happen.

Little scuffles and fights happened at the nice places too, but nowhere near what I was used to. He started telling me I could slang coke and there'd be way less chance you'd get busted. "That's why I have those guys selling for me at those other types of bars and I'm not involved."  It was more gangster schooling for me. He also took me to eat at places I'd never been before, telling me to order anything I wanted.  I looked at the menu and saw things like lobster. I told him I didn't know what to order. "I've never eaten anything like this before."

He said, "Try the lobster, so I did.

"How'd you like it?

"It was good."

"You need to get out of the ghetto mindset. Start thinking and dreaming big. Open your mind to new things." He always had a big roll of hundred dollar bills on him. I was making more money with him. He was very generous, even buying me gold rings. He also taught me how to hide large amounts of cocaine inside cars, in compartments and places that would be hard for law enforcement to find.

I went to customer's houses selling cocaine. One couple wanted an ounce, so Suge and I went to deliver it to them. I sat down, selling them what they wanted. They were listening to the radio and offered us a cold beer. We started drinking with them and doing the cocaine we'd just sold. We stayed until all the alcohol and cocaine was gone. It was getting dark outside and their small kids came inside from playing. I remember telling the couple to turn their lights on inside.

They replied, "We don't have electricity."

I tripped out. "How are you playing the radio?"

"Batteries."

"How are you giving us cold beer?"

"From an ice chest."

Then they started begging Suge to front them some coke. He told them that they bought the last of his stuff. I knew he was lying, he had a lot more. What happened next really tripped me out. This couple pulled out hard hats with flashlights on them, got on their hands and knees and started looking for coke rocks on the floor.

I got mad and said, "What are you doing?

"Maybe some fell on the carpet."

I couldn't believe it. Suge said it was time to leave. As we were walking back to the car, I couldn't help but feel sorry for those kids. They had no money, no food, and their parents were hooked on cocaine.

"Let's go hit up a bar and get some hard drinks," Suge said. "You want a line?" and we both started laughing. He had kilos of cocaine on him, but he wasn't going to give them not one line free. "We sold them their order, did it with them, and drank all their beer. That's a good deal to me."

Another guy called and said he wanted an eight ball, which isn't too much, but we were going to collect some money nearby so we decided to go and deliver it. When we got there it tripped me out too, because this guy had a pretty nice house. When he opened the door he said 'what's up' and we walked in. This guy was a rocker. He had headphones on jamming to rock-n- roll. I told him, "Hey, take your headphones off, we're here to bring you what you asked for."

He did, and then he said, "Hey, I got half the money, but I got some beer and hamburgers."

I got so mad I told him I was going to start kicking holes in his wall.

"OK, kick some right there, next to the other holes in the walls."

I walked around his house, and it was completely empty with holes everywhere. I guess he would punch and kick his own walls with his headphones on, all coked out. It tripped me out so much I didn't kick any holes in his walls. He wouldn't have cared anyway. I gave him the amount he had the money for, and took his whole 18-pack of cold beer. I threw the hamburgers on the floor, and as we were leaving, I said "Don't call us and do something stupid like this ever again. Have all the money next time."

"Could I at least have one of the beers to smoke this with?"

I said no, and we left. He was a crack head. He would rock up his coke and smoke it.

The last story about delivering is about a guy we went to go collect three grand from. We got out of the car to go knock on his door. He came out. I started saying, "Pay up or I'm gonna stab you right now." He was already scared. I was going to pull my knife out, put it to his neck and scare him even more, then collect the money. As I was about to do this, Suge got out of the car and starts telling him, "Look at me. I need my money," and pulled some pictures out of his pocket. He started showing them to this guy one at a time.

The guy said, "Look I have a check, but it's for three months of pay from my job, and it's close to ten grand. I don't have cash on me."

My homeboy said, "I know where to cash it. Sign it over to me and I'll bring you the change."

The guy was so scared he did it. On the way to cash it, I asked about photos. Suge said "The customer's kids at their elementary school, a photo of his mom and some other of his family member's houses."

I tripped out on this.

"Look, Huero, there's a lot of guys like you that don't care out there, but once you show them photos of their loved ones and know who you are, they pay up pretty quickly. That's why I never talk about my kids."

"What? You have kids? I didn't even know."

"Yeah, but no one knows. That's why this will never happen to me."

I was drinking so much hard liquor around this time that it was starting to catch up to me.      I drank a lot, and did a lot of cocaine. I drank so much that I threw up straight blood in the bar restrooms. Instead of thinking I should change my ways, I would go right back out and ask for more shots to drink. Besides that, I was doing so much cocaine, sometimes three or four nights of drinking and doing coke without any sleep, I had episodes when I would just roll around for hours on the floor in pain. My body was breaking down. I was as wild as ever, acting a fool and getting crazy at these bars.

I either wanted to start fights or stab people for the dumbest reasons. One time, one of my uncles and I and Suge were drinking in a bar. Valdo called me and asked where I was. I told him and he came there.

As we shook hands and greeted each other, my uncle fell off a stool. He was sitting at the bar because of how drunk he was. All three of us were drunk, and Valdo was the only sober one. He was just about to get served his drink.

My uncle fell on some gang member's table, and they acted like they were going to get rowdy. I immediately started cussing at them and pulled my knife out. The guys calmed down real quick and everything was cool. When I sat back down laughing, I looked around for Valdo, but he was gone. We hooked up later and I asked why he left.

"I know how you are and how you get. I walked into the bar sober and I had just got out of jail. I was excited to see you, then your uncle falls on that table. I see you pull out a knife and I thought I needed to go. I thought I'd go straight back to jail, but this time for murder."

We both laughed and started partying. Things like this happened all the time. I remember thinking, *"Man, there has to be more to life than this."* Even though I had money, drugs and women, I was miserable.

I went to house parties where many gangs hung out. I took my homeboys from Jackie's with me sometimes. It didn't matter what side of town the house parties were located, I would go and most of the time the people at the parties knew me.

They either respected me or feared me. I had achieved what I said years ago I would be. I'd been beaten up with bats when my dad left and my mom kicked me out. I had become a hardened gangster.

I went to this one party and saw some guys from a gang I didn't get along with. I was with Valdo, Suge, and a few others. I went right up to them and punked them in front of the whole party.

I said, "You know who I am. I don't want to hear you bring up your gang. You're gonna get me beers from the refrigerator all night and if you don't I'm gonna stab you."

They didn't say a word. Then I slapped one of them like a girl, which is very degrading in gang culture. I sat at a table with my homeboys and they were all laughing. I remember later on one of the guys was talking to Valdo about me saying, "Man, your homeboy is crazy."

Valdo said, "Yeah, it's good to have homeboys like that."

Another time I went to a house party and I knew some people there. I went outside and I was drinking with a guy I didn't know. We started talking and I guess my reputation had preceded me, because after talking a while he started telling me, "Hey be careful, because a guy nicknamed Huero is coming to this party." He was talking as if he knew me.

I said, "What? You know this vato Huero?"

"Yeah, and man, he don't play around."

So I started having some fun with him.

I said, "Oh yeah, what does he look like?"

He started to describe me.

"How much bigger than me is this Huero guy?"

"He's twice your size, and he's like 6'3" to 6'4" in height."

I'm actually six feet tall. I couldn't hold it anymore.

"Homes, you're a liar."

"Why?"

"I'm Huero."

He shut up and got scared. This made me laugh. I thought it was comical, so I left him alone.

House parties, or parties of my own was a normal occurrence. I rented hotels and invited homeboys and homegirls over. I filled the tubs full of alcohol, beer malt liquor, bottles of whiskey, and wine. It was just a way of life for me. A lot of my homeboys from the west side, east side, and northeast side would tell me sometimes that when I'd knock on their doors, they would turn the lights off and be quiet until I left. They didn't want me stabbing anyone at their party. I would just laugh.

Later on some of my homeboys from Jackie's told me the same thing. They said, "Sometimes even at family parties we didn't really want to invite you. You're like our brother, but they're our family, and we just didn't want you tripping out on anyone."

I was around eighteen and a half years-old around this time. I wouldn't be free much longer.  I had got my girlfriend pregnant again. I found out I was going to have a son.

25.

## More Trouble and Prophecy

I was still up to no good. I'd been arrested and had been on the run multiple times. I got busted for multiple robberies, assaults, and DUI charges. I was given ten years' probation. Throughout the time I had been out free on the streets, one thing I started doing paying a lawyer. If I got busted, I had good representation in the court system. Up to this point in my life the lawyer had done pretty well for me. But there's only so much they can do for you when you get as many charges and into as much trouble I kept myself in.

I had to report on a monthly basis. Sometimes I wouldn't show up. I would lie to the system about everything. One time I even showed up drunk to report. I talked to my parole officer as if I was as sober as can be. That particular time my parole officer asked me for a urine sample for a drug test. I lied to the guy who was waiting for me to use the restroom. I said I couldn't go, and was it ok if I drank some water out of the water fountain. He said, "Sure." The water fountain was by a door where you could leave the building, so when I pretended to go drink some water I just left and kept partying. I just didn't care about anything. I got into trouble because of that incident.

My life kept spiraling downhill. I got a charge where I ended up in jail. I bonded out of jail immediately. When you have probation or parole you have to bond out immediately or a hold will be placed on you when you're in jail. You can't get out until you go to court, and it could take months to see a judge. This happened multiple times and I guess the system got tired of me. They put out a warrant for my arrest, and this time whenever they caught me, I would not be getting out on bond. The warrant they put out a nationwide warrant with no bond. I was again a fugitive on the run, but this time I wasn't leaving El Paso. I was still selling drugs and hiding out at different hotels that were in the ghetto areas of El Paso. I went to places that charged low prices and did not ask for identification so I couldn't be tracked or leave a paper trail. I lived like this for months.

I was nineteen-years-old now, and the day was coming when my second child, my son was going to be born. I was excited. I was going to have a son, a boy that was going to have my last name forever. The day finally came. I was at the hospital and I got to hold my son. That was the only time I got to hold him and see him for years. The next time I saw my son, he was walking and talking. When I left the hospital that night, I got busted. I was in jail again with no bond. I had to wait months until I went to court to find out how much lockup time I would be facing.

I was the same old me in jail, doing the same thing - thugged out and living crazy. I finally got an offer from the judge. I was sentenced to three months in a restitution center, which tripped me out. I thought I was going to get a longer sentence. I was getting shackled up as normal. I accepted this plea because the court said I would be able to work and give money to my kids, and I would still come out with my ten years' probation. I would still owe the thirty-thousand that I had to pay to the victims I robbed.

When I got there I went through the routine contraband check, and then I went to see the person in charge to go over what I had to pay to stay there and how much money I would be keeping to send to my kids. What they told me tripped me out.

They said, "You have to give us all your money. It goes to this facility and to the probation department. You'll be able to keep five dollars for commissary per month, which is to buy snacks or get hygiene you need while locked up." Then they told me to sign the paperwork agreeing to the terms.

I said, "No way," but not in nice terms. I cussed at them and I said, "That's not the deal I accepted."

"We're gonna make it rough on you here. When your court date comes, we're sending you to prison."

I cussed at the guards and told them to tell someone who cared because I surely didn't. So I was never allowed to leave the facility. I went back into the dorm and I went to shower. When I was getting out two guys came up to me and saw the tattoos on my arm and back and they said, "What's up? You're from PVJ."

"I'm getting into other stuff, but yeah, that's where I grew up."

They told me what gang they were from, and I said OK. I had never heard of them.

They said, "You know who we are," but in a fighting tone.

I said, "Who are you that I should know you or your gang?"

"We have problems with your gang."

I knew they were calling me out, so I said, "They call me Huero, homes, and I'll throw blows with both of you by myself." We started fighting and I beat them both up. So immediately I made my reputation there as someone not to be messed with. After that I would always be punking them. If they had a pack of cigarettes I would take half their pack just to make an example out of them.

I knew quite a few homeboys in the dorm there, and some members of the dominant prison gang that controlled El Paso. Some of the guys there had done twenty years in prison and they were there doing a year to be released.

The homeboys checked out my record. They said, "Ese, Huero, we saw your file of stabbings." I guess they read through my file and knew exact quotes of things I'd said before I stabbed the guys. These guys twice my age, would say, "If someone messes with our daughters we're gonna introduce them to the little homito Huero and see if they want trouble." We would all laugh.

Other guys, including a friend named Mike I knew well from the east side, would tell me, "Man, Huero, do the program and you'll go home."

"No way," I said, "They ain't lying to me or breaking me and I don't care. This is my life."

I messed with those guards, and they messed with me right back. I was so bad there, and in so much trouble, I ended up on permanent lock down status the whole time. I found out I was the first inmate ever to be on permanent lockdown. You were supposed to be able to use the pay phones twice a week, but they didn't let me. I was supposed to get visitation once a week. I think Grandma Rosemary came two or three times, and that was out the window, too. I had gotten into so much trouble that at the time I was there in the late 90s, I had the most write-ups in the history of that facility.

One time we were all cleaning and some of the homies came up to me and said, "Hey Huero, the black vato doesn't want to clean."

I got mad because they looked scared. The black guy they were talking about was probably 6'6" in height and built like you wouldn't believe. I went right up to him as I was in control of the cleaning, and said, "Hey, what's going on? I heard you don't want to clean," and he said, "I'm gonna clean, Huero," and he started cleaning. I told him, "I don't care if you're big. It doesn't mean you can't get stabbed."

So there I was, being a mess up.

I received a letter from my grandma telling me to behave and to listen to rules, and that God's soldiers follow a chain of command. I thought, *"Oh boy, here we go again with this God stuff."* She said she was praying with my grandpa and God gave her a vision that He was clothing me as a prince, and that God was going to use me as a pastor or evangelist. She drew a picture of what God showed her. I couldn't believe it. I thought my grandma was as crazy as can be. I remember reading it out loud to my homeboys and we all laughed. They said, "Yeah right. Huero a preacher. That will be the day."

I still have that letter to this day.

*Excerpt...*

Isaiah, Juan and I have been intensely praying for you, and I have asked others to pray for you also.   I was in prayer today, this morning, and I was speaking in tongues, and I had a vision of you being dressed as a godly "prince"      In today's Bible reading, I read Psalm 43 which reminded me of you.  (read it)   and then I went on to Psalm 44 in which the Psalmist writing it wonders if God has totally abandoned him or forgotten him.   (the way we all feel at times)   But then Psalm 45 speaks about Jesus, how glorious and beautiful He is.   He is a warrior who fights our battles and defends our cause.   He is against evil in every way, because He knows what evil does to His children.   Then I read verse 16 of Psalm 45.   "Instead of your fathers shall be your sons, whom You shall make princes in all the earth"

We got into prayer and I didn't even remember that verse, but when I was praying for you, I got this vision that you were not completely clothed as a prince in satiny flowing robes, but you were being clothed as one, and on your head was a round satin "crown"....

Don't laugh.   What this tells me is that God is going to raise you up to be one of HIS godly "princes"   and He is in the process of making you one, He is "dressing you" gradually, so to speak.   Getting you ready.

And you know, mijo, I don't wonder that being incarcerated there in that tough place is part of the dressing, because it is in tough times that God is closest, and it is in tough times that we learn from HIm, and discover Him to be our Teacher.     It is in the tough times that we also grow spiritually.

In James, it even says "rejoice in tribulations"   (can you imagine rejoicing in tribulations ? ?   Every one says "oh no, how can that be?")     But the Holy Spirit says "rejoice" because if we are submissive to His work in us, He will make us BETTER, by making us stronger, more patient, more self-controlled (self control is one of the fruits of the Holy Spirit)

A soldier is not a soldier until he learns discipline and discipline can be rough.   The hardest discipline is not to rebel against authority, right?   Not to answer back even when the other scumbag is being unjust with you.   But to NOT answer back, to NOT cuss or sass - brings rewards.   It will as surely as there is a sun in the sky.   But it also brings  spiritiual rewards, by making our character stronger to overcome temptations, *& be victorious in all areas of our life.*

Paul in the Bible calls this "the good fight of faith"  .     To learn to hand it all over to the Lord and letting Him handle it is what God wants us to do.   Stop and think a moment.   If I want to handle it my way, God will let me.   But I may very well mess up.   But if instead, I tell God, "You handle it, Lord, I won't." Believe me, HE WILL.

Anyhow, here's the picture of the vision I had of you.   I receive this as a promise of the Lord for you.   Now let HIM DO IT, MIJO.

Let the Lord handle it,   Let Him "dress you"  and prepare you for His purpose in your life, which is good.

*"This is how I saw you, Mijo."*

This is how I saw you mijo.

SATINY crown

satiny robes

I didn't see your feet but of course they are there under the robes

Isaiah, a prince is the
— son of a KING (Jesus)

— has authority
(this is a good one
because we are
talking about
spiritual authority
against the Devil
in the Name of Jesus Christ)

— is a leader
(maybe God will use
you as a pastor,
or evangelist, or
some kind of GODLY leader)

— is an heir
(meaning all his
father's riches +
blessings are his)

— carries his Father's Name
(as a Christian)
+ has given God is your father in you the Name of Jesus Christ
— is involved in the
Father's kingdom
(in some way involved
to advance God's purpose
for people in this
world as well as the
next,

(over)

Romans 14:17 says
"the kingdom of God is not eating + drinking,
but righteousness + peace + joy
in the Holy Spirit"

26.

Prison

I spent six months at this facility. My court date finally came, and they took me there in chains. I waited for my turn to see the judge. I remember the judge holding a file that looked as big as a phone book. I told some of the inmates, "Let's see whose that is." Of course it was mine. They called me up and said to the parole officer that I'd set a new world record for the restitution center.

She said, "Yup."

I had already seen this particular judge three or four times in his courtroom. He was not happy to see me. He held my whole record in his hands, including all my charges, write-ups, and everything else from across the years.

He said, "You're not fit to be in society. I'm sending you to the big house this time. No more chances." The court offered my lawyer a five year sentence, but I would still come out reporting for ten years, and have to pay the victims I robbed.

I told my lawyer to ask the judge if they would give me seven years flat for everything, and let me be released in seven years with no paper or fees.

My grandma and my girlfriend thought I was crazy. They said, "Something is wrong in your head.

I told them, "Look, I know how I am, and I'm just going to mess up anyways." In my mind I figured why not try and see if the judge would go for that.

When my lawyer asked the judge for that deal, he got mad and said, "If he wants straight time, I'll give him twenty years straight right now."

I changed my mind. "Five years sounds real good right about now." Ha ha. I was on the old law system in Texas, so I would probably only end up doing half of the five years. I was already locked up going on a year at this point, so I accepted the deal, and found myself on the way to prison.

Barbed wire surrounded all the multiple fences around the metal building where I'd be spending my time. I thought I'd finally made it. Since I was a kid, it was a place all my homeboys went to. It was college for us, if you will. It's a place where the most thugged out, hard core people ended up. I thought I'd have to be as hard as ever in that place.

The barbed wire gates buzzed open and the guards got in my face, yelling as they gave me the rules.

"We control things here, not you." I spent a while there, locked down until I got changed to the facility where I'd be spending the majority of my time. Barbed wire surrounded this facility, too. By this time, they'd given me an inmate I.D. and number. Then I went to the dorm.

I wasn't far from El Paso so I would be getting visitation, which I was pretty happy about. I knew my grandma would visit me. I saw other inmates' moms and dads visiting them, even at the detention home so many years ago. It dawned on me that not only had my mom and dad never visited me, but they had never sent me a letter, or even sent me a dollar at any facility I'd ever been. That's why I say my grandma's are my heroes.

Being locked up is another world, and you're pretty much on your own. Of course you've got knuckleheads like yourself with you. It was a 50-man dorm. I was showering and a guy came up to me and saw my tattoos. He recognized I was from PvJ. I told him I grew up there. He said he knew my homeboys and he started naming them. He said, "Man, you guys are crazy." He told me a few stories about them and we both laughed.

When you're locked up you have to shower and use the restroom in front of guys. It's just normal in the dorm. Many guys would have to shower together, and a lot of times guys would throw blows in the shower area if they had a problem with each other. There were many toilets butted up side by side. I always tell youngsters, "If you don't want to shower naked with other guys, or use the restroom with other grown men seeing you, behave yourselves."

So this guy and I were talking, and he said, "You had a few homeboys here from Jackie's in this facility that just got out." It didn't trip me out because we were always locked up. My gang was known for doing time and most were in the dominant prison gang that controlled El Paso. This guy tells me, "Hey, I got a joint," and I said, "What? Go get it and let's smoke it." Then he said, "We can't, because the guy controlling the dorm doesn't allow it."

"What? That's stupid. We are all criminals here."

I still hadn't met everyone in the dorm yet, so I asked him, "Are they from the prison gang from El Paso that controls everything?"

He said, "No."

Since I was starting to roll with them, I told him, "Bring the joint. We're gonna smoke it. Don't worry about it." We started getting high. The main guy came up to me and said, "You can't be smoking weed here. It's a rule."

"Are you from the prison gang from El Paso?"

He said, "No."

"Then you aren't controlling things here no more, I am." I asked him what their rules were. Everything else was in order, as far as I could see, but if any drugs came in I told him, "We're doing them." You could tell it didn't settle well with him, but I didn't care. A whole bunch of homies that were there from El Paso started rolling with me. I was making my presence known as someone that didn't care and was down to the fullest for my cause, even if it meant a riot or stabbing or whatever was necessary.

I saw many crazy things at this facility: stabbings, beatings, riots, guards getting attacked, a guy getting hit in the head - his blood flew everywhere. Many times I was the one doing crazy stuff like this and getting in trouble.

One thing that really stands out in my mind out of everything I saw there was about a younger guy I called Kidd. He always got beat up and always got his commissary taken away. He always had black eyes. Three or four guys always beat him up and picked on him. I didn't care. It was none of my business. They would also force him to take his clothes off until he was butt naked and they would spank him with their hands. It was degrading to say the least.

After a few months of this I called Kidd over to my area and asked him why he let himself be degraded like that. "Why don't you fight back?"

He said, "Huero, I do fight back, but they overpower me and beat me up, and take my stuff."

"Kidd, if that's the truth, fight back where I can see everything go down, and tell them, 'Huero said to leave me alone or he's gonna get involved.'"

When it happened again, I saw him fighting back and he told them what I said. The guys came up to me and said, "Hey Huero, this guy told us you said to leave him alone or you were gonna get involved."

I said, "Yeah. Leave the little dude alone. Why don't you do that to me or anyone else that's down? Because you all know it won't turn out the same as messing with Kidd. Next time I see that I'm getting involved, and if I get involved, other down homies are gonna get involved. We will go all out and create a riot up in here against you all."

They never messed with Kidd again, and he was grateful. He would bring me some ramen noodle soups and chips whenever he got his commissary, which I enjoyed.

A homeboy from east side El Paso, from the dominant prison gang I had started rolling with, was in a dorm across from mine. We knew each other from the streets and doing time together. There were windows in the dorms so we could see each other, and we would use sign language to talk to each other. He said he was sending weed to my dorm for me. He sent it through inmates that would clean the facility. He sent me a 20 sack of weed, which was a lot. I couldn't believe it.

We got high every day for a month straight. I was talking to my grandma at visitation. A guy that had just got high in the dorm with me came into the visitation room with his eyes all red. His mom and wife were saying, "You're high." They were so mad at him they left.

There were many ways of sneaking cigarettes, weed, coke or heroine in after visitation. Inmates would take the stackable metal and plastic chairs to another room and layer drugs between. Some of the guards were on our payroll, so they allowed an inmate to take the drugs into the dorms. The drugs would get sneaked in by family members or friends coming to visit inmates. So it was normal to see drug use in there. Before and after they would make sure you weren't smuggling contraband in or out of the visitation room, but there's always crooked guards trying to make some extra cash on the side. All this was becoming more and more normal to me.

Some guys doing time in the same dorm I was in always read the Bible. One came up to me and said, "Hey, Huero. Jesus loves you."

I got so mad. I told them all, "Don't ever tell me that again or I'm gonna stab you. You all are fakes, hiding behind the Bible because you're locked up. I know your kind and I'm not trying to hear it."

I kept getting into so much trouble they ended up locking me down.

27.

Lockdown and Church

So there I was, once again locked down because of always being in trouble. They took all my privileges away, what little I had to begin with. No more commissary, no TV, radio and no regular prison food. I was only allowed to have hygiene when chow time came around. They would give me johnny sacks, which were little brown paper bags. Inside the bags came a bologna sandwich and an orange three times a day. I was always hungry. The bologna in the sandwich was not like one you would have at your house. This bologna was like rubber. You could shake it with your hand and it wouldn't even come apart. Many times it was green.

The guys that cleaned the facility would throw a candy bar under my door, here and there, sent from my homies in the dorms. I cherished those candy bars.

I could still get visits, though, so that was good. I was able to eat some chips and things like that when certain guards were working the visitation hour shifts. All I could do in there was think, read, draw, work out, and count the white bricks inside the room, over and over and over. Week after week and month after month, the guards would come by and ask if I wanted to go to church. I would always say no. The only way to get out of lock down for a little while was to go to church.

I was so bored after eleven or twelve months of being in that room, I just wanted to get out, no matter where I went. This is the part of my story I've wanted to tell the whole time I've been writing.

They asked me again, "Do you want to go to church?"

This time I said, "Yes." My plan was to ask the chaplain what they knew about my life, and to ask if they'd ever been locked up, if they'd ever seen someone murdered or stabbed or shot or overdosed. I wanted to ask them whether they had a mom and a dad, if they grew up with a silver spoon in their mouth. My plan was to mock the preacher, as I had done so many times before at other places where I'd had been locked up. Plus, I wanted to get out of that room for a little bit.

I went to church. As I walked in I saw the inmate Christians pointing at me. I later found out they were saying, "That's Huero, the guy who always picks on us and takes our food and makes us clean."

I walked in and sat down with my arms folded. The chaplain, whose name was Gina, came right up to me. She didn't even give me a chance to speak and said, "Are you Huero?"

I thought to myself, *"I'm Huero, one of the downest homies here."*

She got in my face and started preaching. I remember spit flying on my face she was preaching so hard. She said, "My life was hard too," and she started giving me some of her testimony.

She said, "I'm down too, but for Christ," and she said "I'm from the Jesus gang and I'll die for what I believe in right here, right now if I have to. I'm not scared, just like you. Huero, you need God. I believe you've tried everything else and look where you are. Jesus loves you, Huero. He died for your sins; He hung on a tree for you, and gave His life to save lost souls like you. Your life has meaning to God, and you can do great things on this earth for His kingdom. The devil's been trying to take your life and you're still here. You have a purpose, Huero."

I didn't say a thing. It tripped me out that she was so down for God and had a hard life herself. I had never met anyone like her. Everyone else I had ever met locked up usually just used the Bible so everyone would leave them alone and not hurt them. I would see these so-called Christians back on the streets using drugs and living a lie.

When I would run into these guys on the streets I would slap them and cuss at them. I would tell them, "I'm not a fake, I'm real. I might be messed up but at least I'm real and willing to die for what I stand for, even though it's wrong. You vatos are little girls, scared, and you are fakes. If I ever see you locked up again I'm gonna give you a beating you'll never forget."

Chaplain Gina was different. She was just as down as I was, but for something good. It really tripped me out. I went back to my lockdown room and pondered on this for weeks. Since all I could do in there was think, her words kept messing with me and bothering me.

Around three weeks later I went back to church to see Gina. Her words about this God of hers had me thinking non-stop. I wanted to ask her questions. I knew Jesus hung on a cross because my grandma was always preaching to me. When I got into the church area, the guys would still not look at me, and Gina started preaching at me again. I told her about my dad and mom leaving me at nine-years-old, and everything crazy about the life I lived.

"Didn't Jesus hang on a cross? That's what my grandma said."

"Yes, the cross was made from wood that comes from trees."

That's really how little I understood about this Jesus.

Around this time someone at the facility overdosed on heroin. You could see through a thick glass into the dorm areas. I don't remember if he lived or died, but I do remember guards all around him and the medics there trying to revive him.  At that time in my life I could care less. It really didn't bother me whether he lived or died. I was a heartless criminal. But I remember clearly Gina praying and crying for this guy she didn't even know. It really tripped me out.

She told me, "I don't have to come here to preach the gospel to you guys. There are many other things I could be doing if I wanted too, but I do this because I love you guys, and I want you to know my wonderful Savior Jesus Christ."

 When she said this, the guys expressions on their faces looked as if they didn't like it, but I appreciated her realness and rawness, and her being direct with her words. I'd rather have someone be upfront with me and tell me the honest truth than have a liar acting all nice in front of you, just playing.

Years later Gina told me, "Man, Isaiah, I told God, 'God, I put Huero in your hands because he's crazy.'"

My grandma told me the same thing. Years later she said she would pray to God and say "God, surely if you changed the Apostle Paul you could surely change my grandson Isaiah."

Back to my lockdown cell I went. I have to admit I liked this chaplain Gina because she was down and in your face for what she believed in. I've always thought you have to respect anyone that's willing to die for what they believe in. They stand up for their cause and are willing to die for it, no matter what. To me, if you were willing to die for it, that separated you from the rest.

So Gina's words kept messing with me, and it really made me think. Is this Jesus character real? Is God for real? Did he really send his Son to die for me, for my sin? Is he really that forgiving of a God?

I waited a few weeks before I went back to church again. I was torn between the life I was living and whether God really loved a sinner like me as much as Gina had explained.

I had never felt this way before in my entire life.

28.

From the Streets to the Throne

I knew Gina was going to go off on me again about Jesus when I went back to church, and she did. Later on the guys at the church admitted to me that they would tell Gina, "You're wasting your time on Huero. He's never gonna change."

While waiting in my cell to go to church again, I was thinking hard, and I made a decision.

The next time in church, Gina started preaching to me again. "Huero, God can change your life, your heart, everything about you. Give my God a try. He's not a human, he won't disappoint you. He's not a human that He should lie."

I said, "Gina, I've done horrible things. Will God really forgive me?"

"Huero, Jesus Christ came and died especially for people like you, the worst of the worst."

"Look, all I know up to this point in my life is gang banging, selling drugs, doing time and being a womanizer. I know my fate, and I've accepted either dying on the streets or doing life in prison. That's all I know. I don't have a high school diploma, or even a G.E.D, and I've never been to college. I never planned on meeting someone like you, messing with my mind. But I have made a decision. Look, Gina, if everything you're saying is true, if this God you're telling me about really loves me this much, and really died for me and will forgive someone like me and use this broken life for His Glory, then here I am. I will accept Jesus."

Gina was crying as she said, "Repeat after me, Huero. Say 'Jesus, I ask you to forgive me. I repent of my sins. I ask you to come into my heart and cleanse me. Jesus I accept You as my Lord and Savior.'"

After I repeated the prayer, she said, "Huero, you're saved. Your name is written in the Lamb's book of life."

I was totally free. It's hard to explain, but even though I was locked up, I was free. God touched this sinner's heart. I felt renewed. The first thing I did was ask Gina for a Bible so I could get to know God.

No one in the facility believed I had accepted Jesus Christ as my Lord and Savior. As a matter of fact, word started traveling through the Texas prison system. I found out later guys were telling my homeboys, "Huero is a brother." and they thought, "Yeah, he's riding with our prison gang."

They'd reply, "No, Huero is a brother, a brother of Christ." They told me they would all laugh and say, "You don't know our homeboy Huero. He's worse than us." This was coming from hard core homies that didn't play around.

But the fact was that I was standing for a new cause now, the cause of Christ. I was now a down soldier for Christ unto death, and there was no turning back. Jesus Christ had captivated my heart, consumed me, and I was ready to rock for Christ now, no matter the cost. It's the best decision this sinner ever made. To my God be all the glory forever.

I went back to my room and started reading my Bible but I didn't understand it. So I asked Gina to bring me a kid's Bible with pictures in it to start off with, then I would read the big boy Bible, ha-ha. I started going to church every chance I got and no one laughed at me with my kid Bible because they were still scared of me. I didn't care.

I wanted to know more about my beautiful Savior Jesus Christ.

29.

A Miracle

I read through the kid Bible pretty quickly, and then I went on to the King James Bible. God started revealing Himself to me through His Word. I was excited to know more and more.

Around this time, I was supposed to get more time locked up for my bad behavior, but after a few months the warden himself came to my cell and said, "Blancas, we see the change in you, everyone does - me, the guards, and even the inmates."

What he did next I could not believe. He proceeded to talk and uplift me, which never happens. If you're reading this book and you've done time, you know this is unheard of. Besides telling me how everyone recognized the change in me, he said, "We are dropping your pending write-up charges. We are going to give you a chance and give you work release where you will be able to go to work and come back at night. If you do well, we will release you in three months."

I couldn't believe my ears.

This only made me further believe that Jesus Christ was alive and He was working on my behalf. The warden also took me off lockdown status, so I was happy, but at the same time I actually wanted to be locked up a little longer. I didn't know if I was ready to be free. I wanted to spend more time with God and really know the Bible. I wanted to be able to preach the Gospel. I wanted to know how to answer anyone that would ask me questions about the Bible, or Jesus or the disciples, or just anything about God in general.

It dawned on me how God had saved my life so many times, and how he always protected me, even when I was at my worst, acting a heathen on my way straight to hell. I thought about people who had hits - green lights - on them that I was supposed take care of and how I got shot at so many times and I never died. I'd been stabbed and never went to the hospital and lived. I'd overdosed and lived. I remembered all the bad situations I'd been in, and yet I was still here.

God's hand was all over my life. I could see His fingerprints throughout my life. God was always there and he loved me despite my flaws, despite my failures, despite me not believing in him. I realized God is a great forgiving God, full of compassion, and that God/Jesus Christ had always been by my side, watching over me. These realizations hit me like a ton of bricks. I owed him my life.

I vowed to God that I would preach His gospel fearlessly. I would go where people were scared to go and preach the good news. I was so excited! I was redeemed through the blood of Jesus Christ, and I wasn't going to be no sissy when it came to preaching this gospel.

I liked what I read in the Bible about the Apostle Paul; he was and is my favorite in the Bible besides Jesus, of course, because he was down for the cause. Paul's cause was now my cause. I figured if I lived crazy in the world and I was down to die for nothing, I was going to shift that energy into the kingdom of God. Only I was going to be even more fearless for God and believe and dream bigger than ever for a good cause, the cause of Christ.

I remember coming out to the free world for the first day of work release. I left the facility in a bluebird, a prison bus, with other inmates that were on work release. The bus would drop you at a terminal, and then you could go to look for a job or go to work if you had a job already.

We left the prison at 5:00 a.m. Cars full of gang members pulled up beside us and were listening to loud music. Man, were they drunk. You could tell they'd been partying all night. They threw beer bottles out of their car windows, breaking them on the ground.

I thought, "Oh God, help me stay on track. This world is full of evil. I don't want that type of life anymore. I just want to be a good soldier for you. I want more of you, not the world."

30.

Home

After three months of work release I was free!

I went to see my kids. They were both walking and talking already. They'd made me a sign that said, WELCOME HOME DAD. WE LOVE YOU. Family made a cake for me. I felt so thankful towards my Father in heaven for allowing me to raise my kids the right way from that point on.

After visiting them, I went by my sister's house. I saw a whole bunch of dirty dishes in her sink and I started washing them. I even shined her metal sink. My family laughed saying, "Hey, it's OK, you're not locked up anymore, sit down and relax.

"I guess it's just a habit I have now."

I wanted to find the biggest, baddest church to go to and give half of my money I had on me to God's kingdom. It's funny, but the first thing that came to my mind was to go give money to God's church. I had wasted so much in my past on nothing but bad things. This is when I went to the biggest church in El Paso, the Abundant Living Faith Center. I was so excited to be in God's house.

For the next year, I vowed to go faithfully, every time they had a service. I also started studying the Word more. I read my Bible and listened to sermons from different preachers on the internet. I was getting into the Word five to seven hours every day. I couldn't get enough of it. I traded drugs for God's Word. It was amazing. I loved it. I figured I would study the Bible, go to church, and read godly books that had to do with faith, love, and power - God's power. I was going to do this for one year straight, and then let loose evangelizing the gospel everywhere I could.

I felt strong enough in my new found faith to head back to Jackie's, to know without a doubt I didn't want to live the gangster life anymore, and also to let my homeboys know about Jesus Christ. I wanted to tell them what he had done in my life and how he could change theirs too.

I was twenty-two now, and I was on my way to my hood Jackie's again. I cruised through and a few times saw some youngsters I didn't know. These youngsters started yelling, "West side," and throwing our gang sign at me.

I rolled up and said, "What's up?" and a kid said, "What's up?" but in a fighting way. It was funny to me, because if I'd been the same person I used to be, I would have got out of my vehicle and beat their brains out.

I said, "You know who I am."

He said, "No, who are you?"

"I'm OG Huero from right here, WSL Jackie's."

This youngster's attitude changed completely. He started yelling to all the other homies, "Hey, this is OG Huero, the guy that stabs everyone." He told me his nickname and all the youngsters' nicknames. They said they were from Jackie's too.

I got out of my truck and started talking to them. I remember them going off about gang fights and crazy things they were doing. They brought my little homeboy Tiny up in their conversation. I found out Tiny had got them all in the gang and was schooling them to our ways.

I started telling all these pee wees, "I hope you guys change, little homies, because this life gets crazy. If you guys don't straighten up you're headed straight to prison, man. Check this out. God loves you guys and there's a better way of life for you, all through His Son Jesus."

They looked at me like I was crazy. It reminded me of myself, when older guys would tell me about Jesus.

The kids said, "Are you sure you're the OG Huero we've heard of?" Right when they said this, a youngster I knew came out of one of the project's apartments. I knew who he was because I knew his older sisters who used to party with me.

He said, "What's up, Huero?" and started telling me a story about being locked up at one of the facilities where I'd been locked up. He said, "As soon as I walked in, they asked me where I was from, and I told them Jackie's, West side, and the guys asked me if I knew Huero. I said, 'Yeah, he's my older homeboy." He said that all the guys there said, "'Orale, we take our hat off for your homeboy. Huero is down.' I got respect immediately because of you."

So all these youngsters believed I was the Huero they had heard of. I started preaching the gospel of Christ to all of them. I really hoped what I was saying would touch them one day.

I asked if my homeboy Manny was around. I'd heard he had just got out of prison. They'd seen him around so I kept driving around looking for him, but I didn't find him. But I did find Tiny. He was with a whole bunch of youngsters.

Tiny was excited to see me, and I felt the same. We shook hands and gave each other a big hug.

Tiny said, "This is OG Huero, he's gonna show you what's up. Hey, Huero, show them your PVJ tattoos," and I did. I wanted to pull Tiny away for a little bit to talk to him privately and preach the gospel to him and let him know how King Jesus saved me. But he insisted I talk and school the youngsters for a while. He already had them stealing and doing other crazy stuff. He was tattooing them too. They had PVJ on their necks and arms.

Since Tiny said to tell these little homies what's up, I did.

"You guys need to get saved and know who Jesus Christ is and change your ways before you end up in prison."

Tiny looked at me like I was crazy and he laughed.

"No, for real Huero, tell them what's up."

"Jesus loves you. He died on a cross for you, for your sins, and He came to give us a better life. God is the real deal. I know where you've been and it's not good. Jesus is the only way."

Tiny then said, "Hey Huero, let's talk over here, away from the youngsters. Is this a joke or what?"

I said, "It's not, carnal. I came looking for my homeboys to present Jesus to you all. I've got love for you and I want you all to have a better life."

Tiny tripped out. "Hey, Huero, you know me and all the homeboys respect you to the fullest. I just got out of prison myself."

"Why don't you start rolling with me? I love you and want the best for you."

"Huero, I'm not ready for that. I'm gonna keep gang banging and selling drugs."

"OK, it was good seeing you." We gave each other a hug. As I left, I told everyone there, "God bless you all. Jesus loves you."

I found out some old schoolers from my hood had just got out of prison. They were at some apartments up the block. I went straight there to see them. A lot of the guys from my gang were already dead, so I felt an urgency to tell them about Christ. I really hoped they would listen and change.

I knew for sure I did not want that type of lifestyle anymore. I was totally set free and on fire for Jesus, and that was my newfound purpose in this life. I thought, *"Whoever comes into contact with me now is going to be in trouble, but not trouble the way I used to be, but in trouble because they were going to hear about my King. My sweet precious Jesus, who had set me free, and turned my cold heart of stone into a heart full of love for people who lived just how I used to, or really anyone that needed my Jesus in general."*

I got to the apartment where homeboys were. I walked in and saw my homeboy Koko, and many other old schoolers. They were drinking and doing drugs, a normal thing to everyone and as it once was for me. Everyone was talking about doing time and they were planning on retaliating on a rival gang. They were going to go hit them up. Their plan was to blow up a few of their cars, and if they saw anyone, go at it with them. They asked if I wanted to go and I said no, that I had to leave. I just wanted to stop by and say 'what's up'.

Koko told me, "I knew we would see you again. Some of the homeboys had said you had got out. I knew it was just a matter of time until you came back to the hood."

He said to the rest of the guys, "I told you Huero would be back looking for us."

It's true. I would have, and then participated in the same activities as before. But this time I came to talk to them all about Jesus.

Koko asked me if I wanted a beer and I said no.

"Hey carnal, I'm offering you a beer." He had his hand out towards me with the beer, and I said, "No thank you." I think it tripped him out because I would have taken it from him immediately before. My homeboys were getting so messed up partying, and with the plans they had for later on that night I felt I just had to leave. I was not the same person anymore, and I wanted no part of it. It tripped me out just how much I was changing, because I would have been the first, back in the day, to be down to go hit up a rival gang. I didn't want to preach to them at the time because they were so messed up they weren't going to remember anything I told them about God. I figured I would go back and try later, so I shook all their hands and gave them hugs.

Koko asked me when I was coming back. I told I didn't know, but I'd be back.

Another of my homeboys that had just gotten out of prison, nicknamed Gordo, asked me for a ride and I said sure. He was all messed up too, and he was telling me his prison stories. He needed to go about thirty minutes away, so I started telling him how God saved me when I was locked up, and about Jesus.

"Orale, Huero, you changed, huh?"

"Yeah, man, I'm going hardcore for God."

Even though he was drunk, he said, "That's cool, Huero you know we all respect you, carnal." After I dropped him off, I never saw him again. The last I heard, he moved to Las Vegas, Nevada and got into big trouble. He was doing a long stretch in prison. I hoped my words touched his heart, even though he was blitzed out of his mind.

I didn't go back to Jackie's for six months, but every day until this very day I always pray for my homeboys. I pray that they come to the realization of Christ as Savior. So many of them are either dead, locked up, or living the same as always, but I believe Mark 11:24 (ESV). *Therefore I tell you, whatever you ask in prayer, believe that you have received it, and it will be yours.* This is my favorite scripture in the Bible and I have stood on this verse for many things, including my homeboy's salvations.

A few months later I found out Valdo had been released from prison and his mom had moved to the lower valley in El Paso. I had spoken to him and his mom and Manny, so I went over to their house to say hi and tell them about the change Jesus Christ had done in my life.

Manny was outside in the yard when I got there, smoking a joint with some other guys that lived next door. They were from the prison gang that dominated the El Paso streets. Manny was really happy to see me. He yelled out, "Que rollo, Huero, how you been carnal? It's good to see you!"

He gave me a big hug. It was good to see him. I had a lot of love for him. He was a straight up street guy just like me, but he had such a big heart for those he loved. He was the type of guy that was so down for you. If he had love for you, he would give his life for yours if you got in a bad situation in a street type of scenario. I also respected Manny to the fullest, so I was glad I got to see him free, not locked up.

If you remember earlier in the story, he was one of my homeboys in prison that heard I'd changed and laughed. I got to share Christ with him and I told him exactly what my chaplain Gina told me. I said, "Manny, God loves you and has a purpose for your life. You're precious to Jesus. It doesn't make a difference to Him if you've lived as a sinner. He came and died for your sins to set you free from your past, as he did for me."

I told him how I found Christ, and as I was talking to him about God, I could see his eyes watering. I believe my words were touching him because he knew how I was and how I lived the gangster life to the fullest.

He said, "Orale," to me again and gave me another hug. He said, "My carnal is inside. Go tell him what's up."

I walked in to say hi to their mom, and Valdo and I went into a room to talk. He asked how I'd been and I told him good. I started sharing the gospel of Christ with him. He just looked at me, tripping out on me. He couldn't believe what he was hearing.

"God has set me free. I'm now blessed to be a blessing." I handed him a business card. I'd also started a business and I was doing pretty well.

He looked at the card, mesmerized about what God had done in my life. His girlfriend at the time that had his kids had called him and he answered the phone. She asked him who he was with and he told her, "Huero." She hung up on him as soon as he told her he was with me.

Back in the day, I was always with different girls. My homeboy's wives or girlfriends didn't like their men hanging out with me because of that, and the fact that I was really crazy.

He called her back. "Why did you hang up on me?"

She told him, "You just got out and you're with Huero. You're never gonna change."

Valdo said, "Huero has changed, he found God and he even gave me a business card."

She said, "Yeah, right, like I'm gonna believe Huero changed, and if he gave you a card it's probably a fake." She hung up on him again. We both started laughing.

He said, "She don't believe me that you changed."

We went outside. I had a brand new car and my homeboys were saying, "Man, Huero, that's your ride?"

"Yeah, God's been good to me. He's a Great God." We started talking about our homeboys. Manny asked if I'd talked to Fish.

"Yes, I have." Fish had sent me some pictures of him in prison photos with other guys from the prison gang that controlled El Paso. We exchanged numbers and I told them to call me so they could go to church with me, or to call if they ever needed prayer. I showed them the pictures of Fish. After talking a little while more, I left.

About a month before I had gone looking for Fish. He was still locked up. He had pretty much been locked up non-stop since he was twelve years old. His mom gave me his info after I explained how much I'd changed and how I found God. I wrote to Fish and sent a letter to the prison and gave him my phone number so he could call me from prison whenever he could, and he did.

When Fish finally called me, he asked why I hadn't written or contacted him sooner. I told him the truth.

I said, "I've been locked up a lot myself throughout the years, and to be honest I didn't even care about myself or love myself. I accepted Christ when I was locked up and my life has taken a drastic change for the good."

We talked for a while, until he no longer could, but before we hung up I asked him how I could send him money. We also talked about prison stuff. He told me how he was traveling the world in chains. He was in a federal prison, so Texas was not the only state Fish was in. I believe at the time he was in Louisiana. He told me an OG from Jackie's was at one of the prisons he'd been in. Our home boy was probably ten years older than Fish and I. He was known in our hood. He'd been doing hard time way before us. He was notorious in our neighborhood. He was from the prison gang that controlled El Paso, but had messed up and did something wrong.

He had a green light, a hit, on him. Fish told me he hit him up and said he got all scared. Fish thought it was funny. He also told me about how the guys from El Paso totaled thirty in one of the federal prisons, and had a riot against ninety guys from rival prison gangs.

We got down hardcore and laughed. El Paso is not the biggest city in Texas, but in the prison system El Paso was known as being hardcore. El Paso was known to go at it against anyone, even if we were outnumbered.

Fish did what he had to do against our older homeboy from Jackie's. That was a normal thing where we came from. You would grow up with a lot of homeboys, and a lot of times when you got into prison gangs you would have to kill them if they messed up or did something wrong. I know it probably seems crazy to many reading this, but this is the lifestyle.

I know homeboys until this day that can't be around each other because of this. They would have to kill each other if they ran into each other, which is crazy since we were all from Jackie's and grew up together. But that's the reality of the lifestyle.

What's unique about all this is everyone would still talk to me and show me love. Sometimes homeboys who had hits on their lives were scared to talk to me. A lot of people from El Paso that knew me didn't believe I had changed, but after they spoke to me, they knew.

It was a great situation, and still is because I can preach the gospel of Christ to all of them, which I have always done, and will continue to do as long as the Lord permits me.

Psalms 23:4, "Yea though I walk through the valley of the shadow of death, I will fear no evil for thou art with me. Thy rod and thy staff they comfort me."

Around this time I was preaching to whoever I could, evangelizing for Christ. I passed out tracks with dollar bills wrapped around them at night time. I went downtown to the Segundo barrio area where I once did drug deals. I went over there at night when all the crazy people would come out, and I'd share the good news.

I ran into Koko and some other homeboys there. I hadn't seen him since the last time I went to Jackie's. I didn't get to share the gospel with him and I'd heard from quite a few homeboys that Koko didn't believe I'd changed.

They told me he said, "Unless I see Huero himself, and he tells me about God, I will never believe he's changed."

Some other homeboys from Jackie's came up to me and greeted me. Koko greeted me and told me about how he'd just gotten released from prison. He told me about riots he'd been in with guys from Jackie's and El Paso against other prison gangs. He was so excited about it. I'd heard Koko was sick and close to dying, so I didn't even let him finish what he was saying.

"Are you really sick?"

"Yeah, Huero, I am."

"Look, Koko, you need Christ in your life. You need to change your life around. I love you and want to see you doing good. We're all gonna die. I can die at any time. But now Christ wins in my life. If I die, I know where I'm going. If I'm in prison, I'm gonna preach like Paul. Koko, Jesus has revolutionized my life, and I believe he can heal any disease. I believe one touch from God can revolutionize your life."

"You really changed, huh Huero. I didn't believe it."

"Yeah, Koko, I really changed, and I want the best for you. God can make your test a testimony."

I still dressed the same. I figured why change how I dress. God still loves me the same. God is a patient God. I must say he was working with me and changing some areas of my life little by little, like my dress attire and my anger. I would still think about people who I felt did me wrong, and I would get mad and think if I ever saw them again it wasn't gonna be good. I never acted on what I thought, but I understood I still needed God to guide my steps, not just at this point, but for the rest of my life.

I was praying one day and felt God just wanted me to forgive everyone that had ever wronged me, starting with my mom and dad. I realized the majority of the hate I had always felt since I was young came from the hurt I felt towards them. So I got on my knees and started forgiving everyone. Man, I felt so good after I did. I felt as if a weight had been lifted of my shoulders. I sensed more freedom than ever.

I think God was telling me to release everything to him - to let it go. He was showing me when you hold on to anything not of him, that it only hurts you. I was so excited and happy. God was helping me through the issues of my heart that had bound me for so long.

**Isaiah the Day He Was Released From Prison**

31.

## More Prophecy

A guest speaker was going be at the Abundant Living Faith Center Church, and I heard he was awesome, so I invited a few people to go with me. One was a friend from the east side that was a part of the dominant prison gang that controlled the El Paso streets. I always invited guys that I knew lived the lifestyle I once lived. We got to church and sat down. The guest speaker was Tim Storey, a well-known preacher throughout the world.

I sat there, and as he ministered, God began to touch my soul. I had never experienced a God-encounter like that before. It felt like fire running through my whole body, from the bottom of my feet to the top of my head. I wasn't the only one. My homeboy couldn't even speak. He looked terrified.

Tim Storey has an amazing gift. God uses him to heal people if they are sick. He called different people up at random throughout the whole building, and start telling them exactly what was wrong with them. They were healed by the power of God flowing through him. It was amazing, something I had never experienced in God before.

My homeboy turned his head towards me. "He's not gonna call me up is he?"

I laughed. I didn't care if he called me up. I loved it and it wouldn't have bothered me a bit. I loved the feeling. It was an adrenaline rush. I used to get a rush when I would get all crazy back in the day, doing my gangster stuff. But now it was for God, and it was great.

As I was feeling God's presence, Tim Storey actually looked in my area.

"Hey you, in the jersey, God's touching you.  You're feeling God's power like never before."

I looked behind me and around me to see who else had a jersey on.

"Come on, Bro, who else has a jersey on."

I laughed because it was true. I was probably the only one in the church that had a jersey on that day. I was also wearing black dickie pants and black shiny gangster shoes.

God was dealing with me about how I dressed. I knew he was talking to me, and he was 100 percent right. I was feeling God's presence at a whole new level.

The service ended, and at ALFC Church the guest speakers either have security or ushers or both escorting them because it's a big church.

I watched him as he was going to sign his books for church members (if they purchased one of his books or CD materials). I remember on his way there, when he was passing by me he put his arms out and told the ushers to wait.

"You're name, Bro?"

"Isaiah."

"That's my son's name. Isaiah, God shows me things in the spirit realm. When I was up there preaching, God showed me you. God's gonna use you. I saw you preaching throughout the world. Dream big."

"I believe it, I'm God's soldier."

"I'm serious, Bro, get ready because God's anointing is on you and he's gonna use you."

"I know he is. I don't doubt what God can do. Thank you for coming to the great ALFC Church." Then I went to get my kids in the nursery in the back of the church, and then got in the line to purchase something from this great man of God.

It was me, my kids and their mother. There must have been fifty people in the line, waiting to get a CD or book. He was nice to everyone, saying hi and bye to people. When we got to the merchandise table, he hit the person next to him and said, "That's him," pointing at me. He got out of his seat and walked around the table and came right up to me.

"Isaiah, remember what I said. God told me about you."

"I will."

He asked what I wanted from the table, and I said I didn't know. I just wanted to sow a seed in his ministry. He saw my kids and ex, so he went right up to her, right in her face.

"Do you know you have a great man of God standing next to you?"

She just nodded at him, as if a ghost was speaking to her. Most people get intimidated when they speak to a big preacher, or someone of influence. I never have had that problem. One thing I learned early on was to never let anyone intimidate me. I felt if God is using them, he can use me in a big way too. They are human just like me. The same God that flows through them can flow through me. That doesn't mean I don't respect them or their God-given gift. I've just always felt if you are being real and you can dream with your eyes open, you can be a danger to your enemy the devil, and do big things yourself.

He said to my ex, "I hope you don't lose him. I hope you understand you have a great man of God standing by you."

He told me, "Get whatever you want. I'm gonna sow it into your ministry."

I said, "No, that's OK, I don't mind paying for it."

"No, I'm sowing it into you."

I said Ok and got a book and a few CDs. I didn't want to take advantage of his kindness. He signed my book and wrote DREAM BIG in big bold letters underlined multiple times in marker.

"I'll be seeing you around, Isaiah."

Looking back at it, he wasn't lying. Since that time I've seen him at multiple conferences. When I see him at the great ALFC Church in the back with all the Pastors and Evangelists and godly leaders, he always tells me, "What's up, Perro?" That's like street slang for "What's up, Dog?" like a homeboy.

I've told him on numerous occasions how everything he spoke over my life came true. I even gave him a CD of one of my sermons, which was recorded at a church where we both preach, which is crazy, because he is someone I greatly admire. Until this day, I've also done ministry with people that have attended his Hollywood Bible studies he has in California. Celebrities go to his Bible studies. I'll bring up more about this later.

I started getting invited to preach locally at many different churches. It didn't matter if the churches were big or small. I just wanted to preach about my Jesus.

32.

## Dream Big

I figured I'd done big things for the devil's kingdom, and took it to the limit, so I started dreaming and dreaming big for God. I was watching a really well known evangelist that's always on TV. He gave his testimony and it really inspired me to believe even bigger. He'd been a rocker in a rock band, doing it big in the world. He used to use drugs, too. He got saved and God transformed his life as he did mine. He was very funny, also. As I watched him on worldwide TV, he became one of my favorite preachers. I could relate to him, because the hate I once had in the world had turned into joy. I'm a jokester now and everyone that knows me knows it, but most of all when people have gotten to hear me preach or meet me, they feel the love of Jesus Christ.

I am still down and the real deal, but now I'm down and the real deal for my Savior Jesus Christ. I love God very much, and I want everyone I meet to know. I started speaking about my life, what God spoke about my life in His Word. I started declaring, "I am the head and not the tail. I am above and not beneath. I am more than a conqueror through Jesus Christ."

I started speaking and believing, which is having faith. I told people around me, "I'm going to be on worldwide TV one day preaching the gospel, even at really big churches. I'm going to have a TV show one day. I'm going to be blessed to be a blessing and make great money. With God on my side, I will not and cannot lose. If God is for me, who can be against me?"

I remember people that were in and around my life that were business people, preachers and even some of my own family members making fun of me.

"Who do you think you are? You're a nobody; you're a no one, a failure. You've never even got just a GED, because you didn't attend school. You're a felon. You didn't even have a mom and a dad. How can you do anything great for yourself or your kids? You're a loser. You'll never amount to nothing."

When I would hear this from anyone being negative, I would bust out my Bible, which I always had with me or close by.

"That is what you say about me." Then I would hold my Bible high over my head, open it and read scriptures to them. After I'd finished reading multiple scriptures, I would say, "That is what God says about me. He has spoken over my life and you can say whatever you want, but I will always believe the report my God says over my life." I determined to keep believing and dreaming big.

I got a call to meet a guy to see if we could do some business together. He gave me his address and as soon as I got to his house, God spoke strongly to me. He said, "When you meet this man, tell him your testimony."

*"But then he won't want to do business. He's probably gonna freak out and get scared."*

Then God told me once more to give him my testimony. I knew I was hearing God's voice, so I said, "OK, God, I will."

What happened next tripped me out. Sometimes we just need to be quiet and listen to God's voice and direction and do what he says. Sometimes we just have to shut up and let God be God. He definitely knows what's best for us and He will guide our every move.

I got out of my vehicle introduced myself, and started giving him my testimony.

Instead of him freaking out, he said, "I have TV air time. I have a show that comes out once a week for one hour. I would love if you would come out on my program to preach and give your testimony. I believe it would give many people hope and touch lives for God's glory."

It amazed me that what the God of heaven had spoken to me was coming to pass. As we kept talking, I saw he loved God just as much as I did. Come to find out, he knew my grandma really well, and he had even put her on a radio program years before. He remembered my grandma talking about me and asking for prayer for me on the radio program. I couldn't believe it I thought to myself, *"Wow, look how God works."*

I kept dreaming and believing really big for God. I was adamant to put a dent into the devil's kingdom and save as many souls as I could for God's glory. To me, it's never been about me and having titles. I could care less about that. I just wanted to preach about Jesus anywhere I could to anyone that would listen.

The day came when I preached and gave my testimony on TV. I was excited, not scared or paranoid. I couldn't wait. You would figure it would be nerve-racking, but not for me. You'd have thought I'd been on TV a hundred times. I enjoyed myself so much. I got calls coming in from the viewers that wanted prayer, and many gave their lives to Jesus. It was amazing.

After the program ended and I finished preaching, I thanked God. I was so appreciative to my sweet Jesus. It touched me so much that God would use someone like me to preach His gospel.

In the Bible, the Apostle Paul understood grace because God had forgiven him and used him even though he was such a mess up. I felt the same way. I really understand the grace of God because of his unrelenting grace towards me, despite all the wrongs I had committed in my lifetime.

I asked how much it cost to come out on TV once a week. He told me. I asked if he could get air time for me to preach once a week. He said yes, so I said, "Let's do it." It was expensive, but I figured it would be a good time to flex my faith muscles.

I had gone from a small, one bedroom apartment to a two bedroom apartment, then to a three bedroom apartment. I figured God had blessed me this far, I might as well believe for a house. God blessed me with it. I realized if I don't put limits on God, the possibilities are endless. I believed God would fund the TV program, and I figured since it's His Word, I'm preaching, not mine, He would definitely fund it. He did!

There are so many financial miracles I could write about, but it would be too many. One thing I can tell you for sure is God made the miraculous happen. It was a blast preaching on a weekly basis. I really had to be in God's Word to preach something different every week. I believe God gifted me to do so.

33.

## Chaplain Gina

Around this time I went looking for Gina, my chaplain, the crazy lady that had the guts to preach to me and get me saved. She'd told me the name of the church she attended, so I figured I would go find her and thank her for saving my life and my soul.

I got to go visit her. After the service I looked for Gina to let her know how much my life had changed since she preached to me. I finally found her and she was being her normal self. She was going off preaching to someone about God. I tapped her on her shoulder. When she turned around, she was shocked.

She said, "Huero." Tears started running down her cheeks. I hadn't even said a word yet when she said, "You're preaching, aren't you?"

I said, "Yes Gina, I am." She was so happy she started introducing me to everyone in that church. She admitted to me that she had almost given up on preaching to inmates because she felt no one was really grasping what she was preaching, that no one was really changing. Then she started crying again saying, "Here you are, Bro. You were the worst one I had. I had to put you in God's hands." She was still crying and said, "And here you are, the worst one preaching the gospel. God forgive me for doubting you. Here's your fruit, God."

I was so thankful for Gina. I'm so glad she didn't give up and throw the towel in preaching to inmates or I would have never been saved. Now she always says, "God, just give me one more Huero."

You never know who you're going touch for God's glory when you preach to someone about Christ. I always say it might be the next Isaiah Blancas, someone transformed by the power of Christ, full of faith that's going to preach the good news, that's a danger to the enemy Satan.

Gina has been so faithful to me and my ministry until this very day. I actually had the honor of ordaining Gina into my ministry years after this story. God is a great God that is worthy to be praised.

34.

## Disneyland

I was still with my ex. She would always tell me, "You need to change your life around," at the same time that we both lived crazy and were still in the world. When I was released and this drastic change happened in my life, I think it was too much of a change for her. I think she wanted me to change where I could still be a casual drinker or drug user, but that's never been my personality. I've always been the type of person that goes hardcore, one hundred percent in what I'm going to believe in.

So I kind of knew our relationship was doomed since the beginning, but we had two children together and I didn't want my kids to feel like I did - not having a dad in my life growing up. So I tried to do the right thing for them by marrying their mom, plus I wanted to be right in God's eyes. This was very important to me. The Bible makes it plain and simple not to live in sin to the best of our ability.

I was preaching and evangelizing all the time. God was starting to bless my business also. I wanted to do something special for my kids. I had always heard that Disneyland was amazing, so I started praying to God. My prayer went like this: "God, I thank you for everything you've done in my life. I love you God, and I know you love me too. I know you have good things in store for me and I want to do the same for my children. They are my legacy, Your legacy, God. Please allow me to take my kids to Disneyland just once, so they can experience something I never have." I thanked God and said Amen.

Our theme park in El Paso is so small it's ridiculous. When you go to a place like Disneyland when you're from El Paso, that was something big. I know this because it was also the way I would think before I knew God and started believing God's promises for my life.

I'd had saved up $2,500 and we were on our way. I was so thankful to my sweet Jesus. To me, this was a miracle. To others reading this, you might say 'big deal' but because of the lifestyle I once lived this was nothing less than a miracle from my Father in heaven.

When we got there I thought it was gonna be maybe three times bigger than our amusement park in El Paso. To my amazement, it was much, much bigger. I was excited for my kids but it became an excitement for me as well. I couldn't believe how amazing it was.

It dawned on me that it was New Year's Eve. I looked up to the sky and raised my hands and thanked God in front of people, saying, "God, I thank you for letting me be sober on New Year's Eve, and for knowing You and Your great love for me." I think some people tripped out on me, but I didn't care. I was so happy and felt so blessed. Disneyland was something I wasn't expecting. I have to admit that knowing God and going to Disneyland made me dream bigger than ever. It opened my mindset to a world that was bigger than I knew, and at that time I said, "I'm coming back to Disneyland once a year at least."

After this amazing experience, I watched a worldwide Christian channel in the hotel. I never even knew the channel existed. I was so inspired. The evangelist that I'd seen on the internet earlier in this story that did things on a worldwide level was preaching, and man was the sermon speaking to me. He was speaking about God being a God of overflow and that's exactly how I felt at that moment in that hotel in beautiful California. I felt God's overflow.

The fireworks started going off at midnight at Disneyland. My kids said, "Dad, come out to see the fireworks."

"OK, I'll be there in a little bit." I was so inspired by the sermon being preached on TV that I was glued to the screen. I wanted to see the fireworks but it was not more important to me than God's Word. What an awesome sermon it was! Even though I was having such a good time, I couldn't help but wonder what my homeboys were doing in El Paso, whether they were even still alive or locked up. It always saddened my heart. I wished they came to know Jesus as their Savior as I had.

If it weren't for Jesus, I would be doing life in prison or dead. It always has touched me, knowing my God is such a forgiving God.

When I returned to El Paso from California, I was thinking about how I was sober on New Year's. It really touched me. I'd never been sober on any holiday if I wasn't locked up. I felt good knowing my kids had a good time.

35.

Enemies Turned Friends

I still got calls from my homeboys from Jackie's, and other guys I'd done time with. When my TV program would come on, they would call the number on the screen that would come up for Prayer. One time a guy that I did time with and who had the same nickname as me, called after the program aired.

When I answered he said, "Que Rollo, Huero."

I said, "Who's this?"

"Your twin. It's me, carnal, Guero."

I knew immediately who it was. I asked how he had been.

"OK, still gang banging and selling drugs." He couldn't believe I had changed, as many had not.

"You need to come to church with me and change your life."

He said, "You know what Huero? Anyone else I would tell no, but I will go with you.

"Great!"

A few weeks later he did.

He said, "I saw the TV program as I was flicking through channels and I stopped when I saw you. I told my girl, 'Hey, that looks like a crazy vato I did time with.' My girl said 'Shut up, you don't know anyone on TV,' laughing at me. It looked so much like you, I kept watching, and then I heard you preach, and then your name and phone number came up on the screen. I said, 'Look, that's my homeboy Isaiah Blancas!' I heard you talking about being crazy, and some of your testimony with your sermon and how God changed you. It gave me so much joy to see you doing something good. I told my girl you can preach like that about being a street guy because you really lived it. 'I would know, I did time with him. He was hardcore.'"

He said his girl still didn't believe him, so he called. "You answered."

I could hear him yelling, "I told you I knew him."

I laughed, but I was glad he called. He wasn't the only one. A lot of others called in, including my homeboys from Jackie's. They had actually seen me on TV while locked up, and wrote my number down and saved it. They asked if I wanted to go kick back in our hood. I said, "No, but I love you guys. You are more than welcome to go to church with me or come over to my house and hear sermons, or you can come hear me preach on TV or at churches where I preach."

I was preaching in so many places, that I was no longer going to be in any type of environment that was controlled by my enemy, the devil. If they wanted to hang around with me, it would be me pulling them into my environment, a Godly environment where goodness and mercy dwelt.

I preached at a church in the Segundo Barrio area around this time. As I was driving there, I was praising Jesus because I used to go do crazy things there. Now I was going to inspire God's people. As I preached and gave some of my testimony, I was about fifteen minutes into my sermon when a guy stood up in the crowd.

"Can I say something?"

I said, "Sure, go for it."

"I know you, Huero. I was from an enemy gang. I kind of tripped out to see you here, especially preaching."

He turned to the crowd. "Huero is not lying. He was really crazy. As a matter of fact, if we knew Huero was coming to a party where we were, we would all leave because we were scared of him. We knew one or all of us could get stabbed. If you wanted your party messed up, Huero would be the guy to invite. He was like a dangerous Pit Bull that no one could tame. He was the type of guy that put so much fear in you; he would almost make you pee in your pants."

Then he looked right at me and said, "Huero, I didn't respect you in the streets, I feared you. I was scared of you. There's a difference. But now I respect and you look up to you. I want to be like you."

"Wow! Thank you for sharing that."

I finished preaching then talked with him. He started doing ministry with me on the streets, evangelizing. It was amazing! Someone I once considered an enemy was now my friend and a fellow believer of Christ. God is Amazing. He has never ceased to amaze me. May he always receive all the honor and glory from my life. It's not me, but Him that deserves all the credit for the miraculous change that occurred in this sinner's life.

36.

Making Things Right

Around this time, my dad and I talked, which rarely happened, but since I had found God and forgiven both my parents, I would preach to them about God, too so.

My dad started telling me, "Son, you should leave El Paso. You have a lot of people there that hate you, enemies that would kill you if they had the chance. This was true, but I figured I never backed down or ran from anyone when I was living crazy, so why would I do so now?

"I ain't running from anyone. If I die or anyone kills me, I have a one way ticket to heaven. In the Bible it states 'He will make your enemies be at peace with you.'

How true that is! I'd seen many on the streets at different times that, back when I was crazy, I considered enemies that I had wronged. Some I'd beaten badly, some I had stabbed, robbed, and some I had been locked up with and punked and embarrassed.

One time I saw a guy at Walmart that I had some bad history with. Back when I lived thugged out and crazy, I was with some of my east side homeboys. We stopped at a corner store to get some gas and quarts of malt liquor. I was all messed up on roche pills. That night I was feeling good, dressed up in my normal gangster clothes and some black tinted glasses that had lettering on both sides. One side had PVJ, the other side had WSL, and I had a hat that had lettering in old English letters that spelled out West Side that I'd bought at La Negrita downtown.

As I was walking into the store to purchase my quarts, I'd pulled money out of my pocket and started counting it. The next thing I knew, some guy said, "Hey, you're so and so, aren't you? From so and so gang?"

I said, "No, you have me mistaken me for someone else."

The guy pulls a bat from behind his back and hit me in my head. My brand new tinted glasses fell on the ground, broken in half. I felt my forehead and it had a big knot on it. I really didn't feel it though because I was so messed up on pills.

I looked this guy right in his eyes and said, "I'm Huero from WSLocos, PVJ gang. You hit the wrong person with a bat. I'm gonna kill you."

Man, was this guy scared. He tried hitting me again with the bat, and when he did I grabbed it and started to take it away from him. You could tell by his facial expression he was freaking out. He knew he was in trouble. After taking his bat away from him, he started running and I was right behind him, chasing him and  yelling, "I'm gonna kill you." He ran maybe four blocks until I caught up with him. I started beating him hard with his own bat. I hit him non-stop until he was on the ground convulsing and unconscious.

My homeboys had caught up with me in the car. They were yelling at me to get in the car, but I was planning on killing him. The only reason I stopped was because a light came on at the house in front of us. The people came outside of the house yelling at the top of their lungs. So I stopped and grabbed the guy's head, pulled it up and said, "That's what happens when you mess with real locos."

After I got back into the car with my homeboys, we went to a party and we were all laughing. I showed off his bat with his gang graffiti on it, done with a marker. I showed it off like a trophy. My homeboys said, "Man, Huero, you're crazy."

I found out later from some people that knew him that he didn't die, but I did fracture his skull. He also had a broken jaw, broken arms, legs, and ribs. He'd had to go to a rehabilitation center to function right again.

I told the people who knew him to tell him that if I ever saw him again, I was going kill him. They told me he thought I was someone else and that he was terrified of me.

So I see him at a Walmart. I went up to him to tell him sorry, and how Jesus Christ had changed my life. I was going ask him if he could ever forgive me, but as I got closer to him he recognized me and started running out of the Walmart. I actually chased after him saying, "Hey wait up, I've changed!"

He didn't listen. I couldn't find him.

My pastor friends joke around with me and say, "Imagine the poor guy probably thought, 'He's here to finish the job.'"

I'd never thought of it that way, I just wanted to share my Jesus with him, but I understood what they were saying. He did probably think I was gonna kill him.

Another time I saw a guy at the courthouse that I actually stabbed multiple times. I was there because the law would still mess with me. I will say this to youngsters reading this who are thinking about living crazy. Don't get a record. It's hard to shake a bad record. God will forgive you and use you, but the law and many in this world will always judge you by your past. Please think about that before you start living ignorant. I will also say I'm so glad God is not like humans. He sees the good in us because of His Son Jesus. God is great.

So I see this guy in court, and he was just like me, a real street guy. It could've been the other way around. I could've been the one who got stabbed by him. I went up to him and he says, "Que rollo, Huero," which tripped me out. I thought he would cuss me out or something, but he greeted me. I guess we both knew what it was, and that it came with the lifestyle we both lived. We shook hands and I started to tell him how God had changed my life. I asked him if he could ever forgive me and told him how sorry I was for stabbing him.

To my dismay, he said, "Man, Huero, I thought you were coming up to me to start problems.

I said, "That's the last thing I ever expected to come out of your mouth."

"Yeah, homie, I'll forgive you, and thank you for apologizing to me."

I wasn't expecting that.

"It's good you changed, you were real crazy. You would've been doing life behind bars or dead."

We gave each other a hug then parted in peace. What the Bible says was coming true. My enemies were at peace with me. I was grateful to God for peace being part of my life now.

The next guy I ran into I had robbed without even knowing whose house it was. The truth is, I was with some of my east side homies and we ended up robbing the house together.

I actually knew who this guy was, so if I'd known it was his house, I wouldn't have done it. But what was done was done. I couldn't take it back.

I saw him at a movie theater and walked up to him. He said the same thing the other guy at court said. He greeted me and I returned the greeting. I explained everything. I admitted I was with those guys when the robbery took place, but I also told him I didn't know it was his house, which was the truth. I asked him if he could ever forgive me. I apologized and let him know how Jesus Christ had changed my life. He also forgave me! It felt good inside, knowing I was at least trying to right some of my wrongs, and that God was making miracles happen by touching people's hearts and preparing them for my apologies.

I saw another guy at church. Now this guy I'd really degraded while locked up with him. He was a believer of Christ. He'd tried telling me about God. I slapped him and beat him with a sock that had a soap bar in it, which was a weapon in there. I always made fun of him and degraded him because he talked to me about Jesus.  He also had a high pitched voice, so I made fun of that and called him a girl.

When he saw me he freaked out and said, "Huero, what are you doing here?" You could tell he tripped out because he saw me in church. I explained how God had touched my life and how sorry I was. He forgave me. I couldn't help but feel ashamed of myself, but I also knew Jesus loved and forgave me. Seeing all these people really made me even more grateful to the King of Kings and Lord of Lords, Jesus Christ.

37.

Finding Favor and Direction

My cousin was getting married in Dallas, Texas. I went to his wedding and I think and my family and I were there until two or three o'clock a.m. I got to my hotel around 4:00 a.m. in the morning. At 8:00 I was going to go see one of the biggest preachers in the world. I was so excited. I felt in my spirit that I was going to hear a sermon that would revolutionize my life. I went expecting. I got up and woke up my family at seven a.m. to get to church early. I wanted to see the building and just enjoy the experience of seeing one of the greats. I took my little sister with me. Everyone was saying 'what's the big deal?'

"You'll see."

They were laughing at me saying, "You're acting like a little kid that's gonna get a whole lot of candy."

"That's exactly how I feel."

When we arrived in the parking lot, I jumped out of the car rushing everyone. "Bring the camera!" I took pictures of the building inside and out. One of the security guards guiding traffic said, "You can't take pictures inside. You might as well leave your camera." I whispered to my sister, "Bring it anyways. I have favor on my life."

As I was walking through the church doors I must have had the biggest smile on my face, because the door greeters said, "You're really excited to be here, aren't you."

I replied, "Yes I am!"

The greeter said, "Go to the desk and tell them I sent you so you can sit right on the front row."

I thanked him. When I got to the front desk they said, "Where are you from?" and I said, "El Paso."

They said, "Welcome, you're excited, aren't you."

"I am! Who wouldn't be to get to see one of the greats?"

"Be here in fifteen minutes, and we'll make sure you sit right in front."

I wanted to buy a CD but lines of people were already waiting. It would have taken too long to get in the line and wait with the rest. I didn't want to take longer than fifteen minutes so I silently prayed, "God, I really want a CD of his, please make a little miracle happen for me."

As soon as I finished my prayer, an elevator opened. This church I'm talking about was so big it had elevators. A lady comes out of the elevator and walks right up to me and says, "Would you like to come upstairs and buy a CD?

I asked, "Is there a line? I don't want to miss the preaching." She said there was no line and I said yes. Everyone knew I was excited to be there. When I was buying the CD, they asked, "Are you excited to be here?" but I was so excited thinking about the service, I didn't hear the question. I replied, "I'm from El Paso."

They laughed and said, "We asked if you're excited," and I said, "I'm sorry, yes, I'm super happy to be here."

As I was walking back to the elevator, I heard them talking about me. They were saying to one another, "Did you see the fire in him for God's Word? He's hungry, he's gonna do big things for God's kingdom."

I thought to myself, "Wow, God, you're awesome."

Then God spoke to me and said to me, "You will be preaching at churches like this one day."

I told my family what God had spoken to me and they said "OK," and looked at me like I was crazy, and the truth is, I am crazy, but now I'm crazy for Jesus. I'm not crazy for this world anymore. I'm a radical for Jesus now, and I'm proud of it.

 After this they took us to our front row seats. I was really happy, standing up and looking around in awe. An usher came up to me and said, "Hey Brotha, first time?" I said, "Yeah."

He said, "You have a camera?"

I said, "I do."

He said, "Let me get some pictures of you."

"Cool."

"I'm not supposed too, but you look too excited not to."

I thanked him, and then the sermon started. It was about the blind man Jesus lead out of town to heal him. It was amazing and eye opening. Boy, did God speak to me. I felt it was time to leave out of my town to get something bigger: bigger connections in God, bigger visions, and a bigger mindset.

I prayed, "God, where do you want me to go? I'm not like the young man in the Bible that won't leave everything to follow you. Please open doors and close doors as you see fit for my life."

After intensely praying for around a month, I knew where God wanted me to go. I saved three thousand dollars and I was ready. I thought I had a good enough chunk of money to go where I was headed. Boy was I wrong, ha-ha. I was on my way to San Francisco, California.

38.

## California Ministry

When I got there, I rented an apartment for $1,600 a month. There went half my money immediately. Everything was very expensive in San Francisco, even gasoline. It was almost double the price of gas in El Paso, but still, I couldn't have been more excited to be fulfilling the call of Christ in my life.

I thought about how I used to go to California when I was on the run from Texas law enforcement. *Now it's for Jesus Christ.* I knew I had to get involved with a church immediately. I knew why I was there, and church and God, which go together, had every bit to do with it. I started looking up churches. One stood out to me: Embassy Christian Center. I chose to go there because I like the hotel Embassy Suites. I showed up. I wanted to meet the pastor of the church immediately, or as soon as I could, to tell him why I was in San Francisco, and about hearing God's voice speak to me to go there. I knew it was God-ordained, so after everyone in the church greeted me; they asked me where I was from.

I told them El Paso, and they said, "Oh, you go to ALFC."

I said yes, and then they told me, "Our Pastor is out there as we speak."

I said, "What, in El Paso at ALFC?" and they said, "Yes, he's at a conference there."

This really tripped me out. I thought that it was no coincidence. This is God. After about a week, I finally met Pastor Krishna. He was an amazing speaker and I really enjoyed the praise and worship music too. He also tripped out knowing I was from ALFC in El Paso.

He asked me questions about the pastor out there in El Paso. I said, "He's cool." I didn't know him at the time. ALFC was a big church with thousands of members, but I think
Pastor Krishna thought I knew him like he did because I said he was cool, a good guy.

I was walking by Pier 39 one day, and a guy came up to me and handed me a tract. I accepted it and said, "God bless you." I thought it was pretty cool that someone was out there passing out tracts. I just took it and really didn't look at it until hours later. When I finally did it tripped me out. It was a satanic tract. This made me mad that these guys were promoting the devil and weren't ashamed.

I needed to take evangelizing to a whole new level. I made a promise to God every weekend I was in San Francisco. I was going to be hitting the streets passing out Godly tracts, and preaching to as many as I could while I was there.

I loved Northern California, even though many called it the modern day Sodom and Gomorrah. To me it was beautiful and there was much to do there for the kingdom of God.

Someone told me, "You know, there are witches there."

I laughed at that. I said, "If they want, they can follow me on a boat ride under the Golden Gate Bridge with their chicken bones, and I would still love it." I wasn't scared of that. The life I'd lived was much worse than that. True power comes from Jesus Christ, not Satan. I knew that without a doubt, but when walking by the pier and many other places there, I saw palm readers, gangs, prostitution, pimps, homosexuals, and homeless people all around. I loved it, knowing there was much to do there for Christ. The scenery was out of this world. I would go to Half Moon Bay a lot. It was gorgeous. I would go there to pray and talk to God. I said, "Man, God, if heaven is more beautiful than this, then I know I'm in for a treat."

I walked through the pier passing out tracts. One weekend I passed a palm reader, which I did on purpose all the time. I wanted them to say something, anything to me so I could start preaching the gospel to them. This palm reader says, "You want me to read your palm? I'll give you a free reading."

I said, "Yeah sure, I'll let you read my palm, and what you say might or might not come true, but you have to let me talk to you after you do so. I'll tell you something that will come to pass. It's not a maybe, it is truth. It's a truth that can set you free."

Immediately she said, "No thank you," but since she had started the conversation I figured I was going tell her anyway.

"One day, when you die you will stand in front of God and you will be judged by the eternal court system, and if you don't accept Jesus Christ as your Lord and Savior before you die, you will end up in the lake of fire being tortured for eternity. It's a choice that will forever haunt you if you don't make Jesus Lord over your life. You are accountable because I am speaking truth to you. If you do not accept Jesus as lord you are gonna go to that terrible place, and that is a for sure. It's not a palm reading, the God of heaven will account for the words I am speaking to you this day. Make the right decision.

"I did not believe in God. I was lost like a character in the Bible named Mephibosheth. I told her do research on him. He goes as far to say to King David, 'What am I but a dead dog.'"

I told her Mephibosheth was Saul's grandson and Johnathan's son. Mephibosheth was dropped as a baby and became deformed in his legs. His grandfather and father died in a battle. He ended up in a desolate place where he didn't know who he was meant to be.

"The truth was that he was royalty, just as you and I are. Many times we get dropped by a person or circumstance and the devil will open doors for you to walk straight into as he did in my life. In your case, you're blinded by Satan's lies. That's why you're reading palms. But you cannot hustle me. I used to be a hustler myself. Look, there is great news. Jesus loves you and he's real and he will forgive you if you ask him. In Mephibosheth's story in the Bible, he ends up back at the palace and before they would eat, David would sit Mephibosheth at the table and the tablecloth would cover Mephibosheth's legs so no one knew he was deformed. It's an amazing true story. That's me and you. We are royalty. The devil blinds you so you don't know who you really are in Christ. The amazing thing is like Mephibosheth, Jesus Christ covers up all your sins. It doesn't matter if you have deformities; the blood of Jesus covers them."

At first you could tell she wasn't trying to hear what I was preaching, but as I went on you could tell it made her think. As I left, I said, "God bless you, and true power only comes through Jesus Christ. Get to know him."

I walked to the pier to admire the seals and God's beauty when I read a sign on a booth saying, MEET A REAL LIFE ALCATRAZ INMATE.

I thought, "Yeah, right, a real Alcatraz inmate. It made me laugh. I thought the booth would be packed and there would be a big line to meet a real Alcatraz inmate. Everyone was just walking by, not caring or paying any real attention. To my dismay, an Alcatraz inmate was really there. I couldn't believe it. There was a little line to meet him. The people ahead of me in line were asking him if he would take a picture with them and he said no. I thought to myself that he was probably thinking, "What am I, a spectacle because I was locked up at Alcatraz?"

When my turn came to meet him, I think he tripped out on me because I was so excited to meet him. I said, "Wow, Man, I can't believe I'm meeting a real Alcatraz inmate. Did you ever think you were gonna be famous from doing time?"

"Not in a million years."

"How big were the cells, and who did you do time with?"

He wasn't talking to everyone else much. He was selling a book he had released and he wasn't even signing the books. I think when he saw me so excited to meet him he opened up a little bit. I thought I would connect with him on some street stuff like I do when I talk to homies on the streets.

"I've been locked up too, my whole life in and out until I found Jesus. Do you know Jesus too?"

"I do. I actually talk about it in my book."

"You found God in prison?"

"No, I accepted Jesus in my heart when I got out. I didn't want guys saying I used God's word as a crutch or because I was scared."

I understood him completely. I lived the same way back in the day. We started talking about places where we'd done time and the conditions we were both in. He talked to me quite a bit and even started laughing and smiling. He could relate to me. I wasn't just someone trying to get a signed book anymore. I was an ex-inmate that had changed, just like him.

As we talked he said, "You don't want to get a book? I'll sign it for you."

"How much are they? I would really love to but I'm low on funds. San Francisco is way more expensive than Texas, and it's been raining a lot so I haven't been able to work as much as I want. It's been an honor to meet you. God bless you, and I'll be praying for you. As I walked away, I turned around and said, "You know what? I'll buy your book. I'll never have this chance again." I took one.

He laughed and said, "Let me see your book," and he signed it. He wrote the years he was in Alcatraz and his inmate number. It was pretty cool then he said, "If you have a camera I'll take some pictures with you."

I ran across the street and bought a $5 disposable camera, and then squatted down by him sitting down on his chair like a prison style photo. In the photos I took you can see him serious in some photos, and some with him smiling slightly. I thought after the experience how cool it was, and I thought Gods favor was all over my life.

I was able to visit my grandma a lot which I enjoyed very much. I always preached to her. She said, "It's good you've changed, but don't be a fanatic."

I'd laugh. I stayed at her place and she would work nights to early morning. I waited up for her to make sure she got home safe. She rode the Amtrak to work and back. She was never big on owning a vehicle. This one night she was late and wasn't answering my phone calls. I thought, *"No one better have done something to my grandma. It won't be good for someone if they do."* As I thought this, my grandma walked in the door.

I started going off, saying, "Where were you? Why weren't you answering my calls? You had me worried. I was gonna go looking for you?"

She yelled at me. "What's wrong with you? My phone was ringing non-stop. It was embarrassing. Who do you think you are?"

My dad and I started laughing, and then we hugged each other. As I said before, my grandmas are my heroes. It's a memory I will never forget. My grandma from California was a Catholic and had not accepted Jesus in her heart. I always told her she needed to.

I'm not religious. I've have never fought with anyone about God. I believe that is a big problem. I don't care what denomination anyone stands for. All I care about is that they know Jesus Christ as their Lord and Savior. I believe many will be shocked in heaven when they see who else is there. I've always felt we are all family. If you're a believer, we should act like it here on earth, because all that nonsense will not exist in heaven.

We will all be family in heaven.

39.

Forgiveness

Around this time, I got to go eat with my dad at a restaurant. We had a heart-to-heart talk. He told me how sorry he was for leaving me when I was nine, and how he felt guilty all these years because of it. As he spoke, tears rolled down his cheeks.

"I forgive you and it is not all your fault. There are many that had lives like mine that have become teachers, doctors or lawyers, or did something great with their lives. I chose that life style."

He said, "Son, you were only nine."

"I know, and at that young age I made up my mind who I was gonna be and chose the wrong path. The God of heaven had a plan for my life and he was always there protecting me."

We made peace that day. I know we had a long way to go at that point, but God was working. A lot of people were still mad at my dad and holding grudges and resentment towards him. They would tell me not to forgive him, that he wasn't worthy of my forgiveness.

I would remind them that if *I* let it go, why are *you* holding onto it? "You let it go too. Christ has forgiven me and I don't deserve forgiveness either but He loved me even though I was a horrendous sinner. God is our Father and if he sent Jesus to die for us while we were all sinners, who am I to hold hate in my heart and not forgive? God's love set me free. I don't live in anger and hate anymore. Forgiveness and love are in my heart, mind, body, and soul now."

40.

Miracles on the Pier

I had been in San Francisco around four months. I would be there six months total. I passed tracks out in the San Francisco downtown area. I only had twenty dollars left to my name. I'd exhausted all funds. I was eating crackers before going out to preach on the streets and breaking my last $20 into one dollar bills because I put a dollar on each track. My ex and kids had been with me, but they went back to El Paso. They were waiting for me to send them money from working when rains stopped in San Francisco. It seemed it would never stop, but I was not detoured from the mission I was on for God. I always said to myself, "Soldier up. If I'd been a street soldier in the world for the devil, I was going to be even more intense for God, even if I had nothing and was hungry." It was all good. This mindset God has given me has separated me from most.

The first guy I gave a track with a dollar was homeless and entertaining people that walked by him to make a buck. I walked up to him and gave him a track with a dollar bill in it and said, "God bless you, my brotha. Jesus loves you."

He came running after me and said, "Hey, bro, thank you."

I told him he was welcome.

He said, "You don't have to pay people to reach them with the gospel."

I said, "It's only a dollar, Man. It's just so you could get a small cup of coffee or something."

We talked about God for a little then he put his hand in his pocket and said, "You're awesome," and gave me five bucks. "I want to sow it into your ministry. Go buy some more tracts. We need people like you out here."

It touched my heart that this homeless brotha had given me money to evangelize. I thought, *If a homeless guy is giving me money, I must be doing something right.*

The next guy I gave a tract and dollar to said, "You should think of giving Bibles out. Do you think I'm poor because I'm out here?"

"No, I don't judge anyone."

"You are right, because I'm not poor; I'm rich because I know God too." He started quoting scripture and preaching to me. "You're not from here. It's not your time yet to be here. I know you love it here. God knows your heart, but you need to go back where you're from and touch people who live the way you once lived."

This tripped me out. There was no way he could have known if I was from there or not. If you've ever been to San Francisco, it's a very diverse city with tons of cultures and different races.

Then he prayed for me. After that I said, "I'm parked only two blocks away. I have a Bible in my car. I'm gonna give it to you." I left running to get it. When I got back with the Bible, I looked everywhere for this man, but he was nowhere in sight.

There was a little corner store on the street and I asked the guy inside, "Hey, did you see a really big guy leave, running from here?"

"No sir, there was no one here."

I'd returned so fast, even if he was running, I would have seen him. Then it hit me. This was no man. It was an angel of God prophesying to me. I knew I'd had an encounter with an angel. Unlike many out there, I have always believed the impossible and moved towards that. I know that during those times when people break down and give up on life, the enemy is attacking harder than ever because a breakthrough is right around the corner. If we will only stand and believe and trust God, miracles are going to come in clusters.

41.

Choices

Now around this time I was in constant prayer, praise and worship, and in God's Word. I had to have the full armor of God on my life. I was praying for financial miracles and for God to show me why he had sent me to San Francisco. Little did I know he was about to reveal everything really soon and it was gonna be bigger than I could ever think or imagine. I had been to every service faithfully at Embassy Church and always gave tithes and offerings no matter what I was going through. I understood how important my giving was to God's kingdom.

Pastor Krishna and I became pretty tight, which was amazing because I really admired him. He was and is a blessing to be around. God told me I was going to preach at Embassy one day, which was awesome. You have to realize the speakers Pastor Krishna featured at his church were no small timers. They were and are, until this very day, cutting edge preachers who impact the world for God's glory in one way or another.

I never told Pastor Krishna what God had told me. He probably would have thought to himself, *"Yeah sure, OK buddy, ha-ha."* But I knew what God had spoken.

The rains calmed down and I was able to work and was making pretty good money. I'd placed ads out in the newspapers providing services so I could make extra money. This is when a man called me and asked if I was Isaiah. He saw my ad and wanted me to come to his office in Hillsdale, California.

"I want to talk to you. I'm the owner and I have never called anyone from an ad before, but there was something about your ad that made me call."

I thought, *"Yeah, it was God."*

He said to come over and ask for him, and then hung up on me.

I thought, *"This guy acts like he's rich,"* and boy was I about to find out how rich he was. When I went to meet him at his office I asked one of his secretary's for him. I explained how he called me and wanted to meet me. This tripped them out.

They said, "That's odd. He never calls anyone. As a matter of fact, people call him non-stop trying to get a hold of him and trying to set meetings up with him to do business with him. He doesn't give them the time of day."

They took me to his office. I had to go eight floors up on an elevator to get to his office, which was beautiful. He stood from his chair and said, "Isaiah."

I said, "Yes sir."

He greeted me, shook my hand, and said, "Have a seat. Where are you from? Tell me your past, where you are now, where you believe you're going in the future and be honest with me."

So I said OK, and I told him everything about my past and why I was in San Francisco. I told him where God was taking my life. When I finished speaking and telling him what he wanted to know about me, I said, "Where God is taking my life is not a maybe, it's a for sure thing. My faith and belief is unwavering. I don't just think; I know where I'm going."

He sat back in his chair puffing on a big fat cigar. He wore a big gold ring with humongous diamonds. I thought his ring was more expensive than the house I had in El Paso. After puffing on his cigar a few more times, he said, "Isaiah, you remind me of me when I was younger."

I said, "Wow, I really would love to be at the point you're at in your life."

"Isaiah, I own this building and many others just like it throughout the state of California. They're mine, paid in full. Come with me, I want to show you something. Tell me what you think."

We went into another room where he showed me a new product he was putting out in the market. He was a major distributor in his line of trade, and did I mention he was a billionaire?

I told him it was amazing.

"Isaiah, I need hungry young men like you on my team that dream and dream big, that aren't scared to take risks." He asked if I wanted to jump on board with him and his company with full time contracts.

"I'm making some money now, and I just started too. I'd need some money."

"How about this? How about I give you three grand cash right now, and I buy you your own brand new truck in your name."

"Let me pray about it," I said.

"Don't make me wait too long."

I met with him two more times. The next time we met he said, "What if give you five grand and the truck?"

I again said, "Let me pray about it." The third time we met he had a better deal for me.

"Look, Isaiah, I really want you on board with me. I found out you love San Francisco." He had actually got in contact with people I knew and they told him I loved California.

"What if I give you ten grand, the truck, and I buy you a three-bedroom house in Northern California. I'll put the title in your name."

"I don't know."

"Isaiah, I can promise you within a year of being with me you'll be a millionaire."

"Give me three days to think about it."

"Three days and no more. I won't call you again."

Owning a house in Northern California has always been a desire of my heart and there was nothing more I would've loved than to live in California. Anyone who really knows me knows that I love California, especially Northern California, but this was my problem. If I worked for the rest of my life, long hours every day, I could not preach the gospel, which was worth more to me than any house or amount of money anyone would offer me.

I told God, "This is a great opportunity but I can't accept this. I won't be able to save souls for your glory."

Then God gave me a thought. The thought was a baby crying and a parent giving the baby a toy or rattler that amazed and amused the baby. I thought of us humans. We are the same way. We can be down in life sometimes, and if the devil gives us a new car or lots of money we are amused. Also, I remembered the verse in the Bible, 'What does it profit a man to gain the whole world and lose his soul.' (Mark 8:36)

I am not against anyone having money. Money in the right hands can do amazing things, and for anyone preaching the gospel money is a tool. I believe God just doesn't want money having you. So I'd made up my mind. The choice was clear. I was going to keep preaching the gospel of Christ. I felt I owed Jesus more than that. He had radically changed my life.

I'll remind you I needed the money at this time in my life, but I wasn't going to sell out at any cost. I would rather be in a cell, broke as a joke for the rest of my life knowing I was going to heaven than to have everything and go to hell. Even at that age I understood that life is tough, and it's like a roller coaster sometimes. You're up and sometimes you're down. The only
solid thing is what you stand on and if that is the foundation of Christ, you're good.

I always tell myself until the present day, "You're a soldier for Christ, Isaiah. You might bend, but you will never break because the God of heaven is on your side. With Jesus Christ on your side, you can't lose. You are dangerous to your enemy the devil. You have that Apostle Paul type faith."

I called Jacob, my brother in Christ who went to Embassy Church, who was and is a protégé' of mine. I liked Jacob from the first day I met him. God had given me words to speak into his life which I still do. God had opened Jacob up like a book to me. I have always spoken life into his life. I called him and explained what was going on and the opportunity that had come about with this man.

He said, "Wow man, what a blessing. So you're getting a house out here."

I told him the thought God had given me about the baby with the toy. "I turned the opportunity down."

This is not the last time an opportunity like this would pop up within the years to come, and many friends I would make in ministry would always say, "Wow, Man, that's amazing."

There are very few who would turn down opportunities and money like that.

I had been in San Francisco going on six months. I would be back in El Paso very soon. One day I prayed for hours and I heard God's voice say, "It's time to go back to El Paso. I'm going to bless you there. Go back."

I said, "OK," and let Pastor Krishna know that I would be going back to Texas and that I'd attend one more Sunday service before leaving.

Pastor Krishna did something nice for me on my last visit that I was not expecting.

42.

## This is My House

When I got to Embassy the Sunday before I left, Pastor Krishna called me up to the pulpit before the service started to let everyone know I was leaving. He prayed for me and told everyone how faithful I'd been while there. I really appreciated what he did for me. It was amazing.

I told everyone in El Paso I was headed back. They wanted to know why because I'd finally started to make money in San Francisco. My family wanted me to stay there and make some money, then come back. I let them know that God told me to go back and watch him work.

When I got back, a storm had come through El Paso that left homes flooded and really damaged, which was a very rare occurrence. I had so much work that I recouped all the money I had lost in San Francisco pretty quickly.

I believe I went to San Francisco to get connected to Pastor Krishna. It was God ordained.

Around a month passed in El Paso, and I'd been believing God for a home. I was staying with family while looking for a home. When I was in San Francisco I told everyone including Pastor Krishna, "Man, they're building me an amazing brand new, two-story house. It's almost ready for me to move in."

He would say, "I have to check it out when I go back to El Paso."

The fact was when I was out there, I was broke, but a bigger fact and reality to me was I believed in God's promises. I believed more in the unseen than what you could see with your physical eye. I was seeing through spiritual eyes and I never had more faith in what my God could do on my behalf. I believe it was 2003 or 2004.

I talked about this two-story house around my ex and my sister. My sister thought I had lost my mind like our mom. She even asked me if I wanted to go see a doctor to see if everything was alright with my mental health. I laughed at her and said, "I'm not crazy. I just really believe God's promises for my life. If anything, there's something wrong with people who don't believe like I do."

I was driving around one day and saw a two-story house and just like I said; it was under construction. It wasn't finished yet. I walked in and by chance the realtor was there. She asked me if I was interested in the house.

"This is my house."

She laughed at me.

I went upstairs and placed my hands on the walls and said, "Jesus, everyone has been laughing at me. They even think I'm crazy because I believe in your promises. Show them you're real, Jesus. Show them you could bless even someone like me from the ghetto. Let them know that anyone who trusts You can be blessed." I prayed over the house, claiming it as mine, knowing that Almighty God heard my prayers.

The realtor heard me pray. After I finished she asked if I had good credit.

"No, I don't. I messed it up living in San Francisco, but God has spoken. This house will be mine."

I think she tripped out, but she said, "Come down to my office and fill out paperwork on it anyway."

I did.

She called me after the paperwork was submitted and said, "Isaiah, I can get you into that house, but you're going to need so much money down and you have to have it within three days."

"I'd been saving money and was still lacking around five thousand dollars. I had three days to come up with it. It was time for God to move and make a miracle happen.

I prayed and believed my God as I had so many times before. When the three days were up, God had made it happen for me. I had what I needed to get the house.

My ex said, "What about the furniture?" She said this because our furniture had been in storage while I was in California. The flooding in El Paso had ruined our furniture. Now this seemed to be a problem for her, but not to me. God had already done so many miracles in my life. I didn't doubt what my God could do.

When I closed on the home, the realtor said to me, "Oh yeah, guess what?"

"What?"

"You keep that extra five thousand. We didn't need it after all."

I thanked my sweet Jesus. "There's our furniture." I can still remember going into the house. It had 24ft ceilings, two living rooms, a double garage, a Jacuzzi in the master bedroom besides the other rooms. It had remote control ceiling fans. I laid down in one of the living rooms looking up at the ceiling. I was in awe of God and how good he was to me.

I thought, *"Wow, is this really my house?"* I remembered my youth and having nowhere to sleep at night. I began to praise God with tears running down my face. I thought this type of blessing was for rich people, not someone like me. I will never forget that day.

43.

## My Mentor

Pastor Krishna called me. He said, "Isaiah, God spoke to me and I want to talk to you in person." He asked if I could fly out to San Francisco to meet with him. He even offered to pay for a plane ticket, but I was doing really well and I told him not to worry, I would be there.

My faith had become known to many, and many looked up to me. I was getting invited to preach at many places now. One thing I needed in my life was a mentor. I understood that you cannot be a man of authority if you were not a man under authority. The Bible was very clear on that issue. So off to San Francisco I went.

Pastor Krishna was there to meet me when I arrived. We talked for a little bit, and then he dropped me off at my hotel. He let me know he was picking me up later to take me to eat so we could talk about what God had told him.

The restaurant amazed me. It was a beautiful and right on the ocean. I was so excited to be back in Northern California, especially with Pastor Krishna. Jacob joined us. Pastor Krishna ordered all types of food. The table was a big circle table that would spin around so you could try the different foods. There was duck which I had never tried, seafood and many other upscale dishes. You could see the ocean through big glass windows.

Pastor Krishna said, "Isaiah, you have many who look up to you but you do not have a strong solid voice from a man of God speaking into your life. How would you feel if I became that voice and start mentoring you?"

It was exactly what I needed in my life.

"Pastor Krishna, I would be honored if you would do so."

Now it was time to get groomed, so to say, in Gods kingdom. This time it wouldn't be by a drug dealer. It would be through a great man of God whom I had the utmost respect for. From that day on, I picked Pastor Krishna's brain and asked him all types of different questions.

Every time he would laugh and answer all my questions. I couldn't have been happier. I was hungry, as always, to grow in Gods kingdom.

After dinner, Jacob got up and said, "Isaiah, I got you a 100 percent wool jacket from the mall." He got up and put the jacket over me. It touched my heart so much.

I couldn't help but think, "Wow, God surely knows what he's doing." I felt like Joseph in the Bible getting a jacket and feeling favored. I never really had a father figure but I had a spiritual father now that loved me and wanted to work with me and help me grow in God and in life. Jacob had even given me some money.

Pastor Krishna and I have had many talks since then. One time years later I took him out to eat in El Paso and we were taking about when I'd gone out to San Francisco.

He said, "Isaiah, it didn't work out for you in California did it?"
"Yes it did."
"But you didn't make it out there."
"True, but God had a plan because you mentor me. I'm sitting here with you."
He laughed and said, "You got me on that one. I am here with you."

I laughed too, because I almost never got one up on Pastor Krishna. He is as sharp as they come, a very Godly, very wise man. I am honored that he is in my life. Pastor Krishna has always believed in me and has always seen the good in me. I will always give him the place to speak into my life as he sees fit. I know he loves me and wants the best for me. He is the father figure God placed in my life.

To anyone reading this book; if you never had a father, know that God is your Father and He loves you and wants the very best for your life. Sometimes God places someone like Pastor Krishna in your life on this earth to fill a void. Hear my heart as I say to you: God has great plans for you, and the voids you need filled - He will fill.

I went back to El Paso much inspired. God was doing more for my life than I ever dreamed, and he was just getting started.

44.

## My Hero Goes Home

I received really bad news about my grandma from California. I found out that she had cancer throughout her body and only had a few weeks to live.

This really tripped me out because my grandma from California was very healthy. It was hard for me to swallow. I understood why God had me go to San Francisco. It was not only to get connected to Pastor Krishna but also to allow me to spend time with my grandma when she was healthy. As I've said throughout my story, my grandmas were my heroes. When my mom and dad left me, my grandmas became my parents.

I was heartbroken. This was the hardest thing I'd dealt with while walking with God. I flew out to California to spend time with her before she passed. When I got there, she looked pretty good so I decided to visit the ocean. My dad and other family that were there tripped out that I would do that. They called asking me why I left.

I told them that Grandma looked good. The truth was that it was hard for me to come to grips with my grandma being sick. I was devastated. I just didn't want to break down and cry in front of my grandma. I was supposed to be this faith filled warrior but it was hard to bear. I wasn't gonna have her around. My grandma in California is someone I could call and go to with my problems and issues of life. That was something very rare for someone like me to have.

When I returned from the ocean, I didn't leave again until she passed. I'd bought her favorite candies while I was out, which were red hot tamales, even though she couldn't eat them. I wanted her to know I cared and to see the candy nearby. I also got her a little toy trolley. She loved riding trolleys in San Francisco. This toy trolley would sing music. She'd ask me to
wind it up for her to hear it play. I have to admit I have never really cried. I've always been a man's man, but when I would play the music from the trolley, it was very hard for me not to bust out in tears right in front of her. I tried to be as strong as I could for her and the rest of my family since I was the one who was riding with Jesus. It was hard to keep it together.

I'd brought a DVD of a worldwide Evangelist, the one I've brought up in my story. On this DVD he tells of having seen and been in heaven. It's one of my favorites. I played that video over and over. It brought peace into the atmosphere.

My grandma's stomach had gotten so big and round in a matter of days that she looked pregnant. It was the cancer growing. My beautiful grandma joked, saying, "I look pregnant, huh? I look horrible."

I'd say, "Grandma, you look beautiful as always."

She was so strong, and she never complained. I didn't think I could even be as strong as her in that condition. I thought, *"My grandma's a straight up warrior."* I was so glad she got the chance to see me change my life around. I was grateful to God for that.

I told her, "When it's your time to go to heaven, tell Jesus, the Apostle Paul, and all the disciples that I can't wait to meet them. Tell them I'll see them soon."

I'd lead my grandma to God. She had accepted Jesus as her Lord and Savior, so that brought peace to my heart. I wanted her to sit up and she said, "Help me," and she hugged my neck and hung onto me for a while. She asked if I was tired of her hanging on my neck, and I was a little bit, but I said, "No, Grandma, I could let you hang around my neck forever."

She said, "Bring your ear to my mouth so I can tell you something."

When my ear was close she whispered, "You've always been my angel. I love you."

This broke my heart. "Grandma, I need to use the restroom." I cried like a baby in the bathroom. I would have given my life for my grandmas. After crying for a while, I wiped my tears and acted like nothing was wrong.

Not long after my grandma died, we buried her in Half Moon Bay in Northern California. It was her wish. It was the hardest thing I have ever had to do. It broke my heart knowing I would never be able to call and hear her beautiful voice again, or see her waiting outside of her place in California waiting for me to arrive from Texas.

I knew it was a sickness sent from the enemy to kill her. In the Bible it states that God came to bring life and life more abundant. The devil only comes to kill, steal, and destroy. I was not mad at God but at the devil. I was going to hit the devil big time for this. I was going to hit him where it hurts, where he had strongholds.

My grandma was in heaven now and she was no longer in my past, she was in my future. It gave me great satisfaction knowing this truth. I decided I was going to hit the devil's kingdom in one of the most dangerous places on earth. I would start preaching the gospel of Christ hardcore in Juarez, Mexico. It was time to soldier up for the King of Kings and Lord of Lords. It was time to make a dent in the enemy's camp.

I was one man willing to make a difference and bring some hope, but so was Jesus one man sent by God, His only son. Paul was one man. King David was one man that stood up for the cause. Joseph was one man. There are countless revolutions that were started in the Bible about one man standing up against the enemy. I understood this and I was one man willing and ready to stand for the cause of Christ. I was, and am, an excited man on a mission. It was time to do some hardcore ministry.

45.

Back to Mexico

Juarez, Mexico was a place no one wanted to go to. For years I would try to get fellow believers in Christ that went to different churches to go with me, and every time I would ask they would look at me as if I was crazy.

"Oh, no! We will not go to Juarez."

I would laugh at them and tell them not to be little girls, ha-ha.  I would say this in love, but I was frustrated by how passive believers were about spreading the gospel.

David in the Bible said, "Is There Not a Cause?"  I would ask God, "Where are all the hardcore warriors like the Apostle Paul and the disciples that weren't scared of doing time in prisons for Your namesake, risking their lives or even dying for the gospel?"

I started praying for connections that were hardcore just like me that wanted to hit the enemy where it hurt him. God heard my prayers. I started getting connected to churches and ministries in Juarez.  Juarez has always been a really violent mafia/gang/cartel controlled city. Everyone from cops to government officials out there is very crooked. Almost anyone and everyone can be bribed there. It's a very big difference from the United States.

I started preaching at churches in Juarez, big and small. Some had two to three people, sometimes others were mega churches with 800 to thousands of members. It didn't make a difference to me, as long as I could preach the gospel. I also started doing street ministry in the red light district area which was full of bars, clubs, prostitution, drugs, and gang violence. I would go out from around midnight to 3:00 a.m., when it was the worst time to be out. Most thought I was crazy but I loved it. Unlike other people, I felt totally normal being out there. It was an adrenaline rush for me. I knew I was making an impact for God's kingdom, and I had never been more excited about doing ministry in my life.

I will share a few things I saw while doing ministry in the red light district in Juarez. I saw a young kid that couldn't have been older than ten that was a full blown heroin addict. He had tracks/scars over his arms from shooting heroine so much. He was dosing off as I had seen my homeboys do in the Jackie's projects so many times from being so messed up on dope. It wasn't new to see a heroin addict, but never before a kid so young. It was crazy. Man, I could definitely see I was preaching the good news where they really needed it.

The older guys would hook young kids on heroine so the kids could do their dirty work, such as stealing from stores or robbing houses or hustling people that would come to Mexico from America. It was sad.

Another time I saw a girl who was twelve coming out of a club. She was drunk on heroin and she was pregnant. It was crazy but just another sad story from Juarez. I saw a very poor neighborhood not far from that area. Kids were eating after cows and pigs. They would eat the leftover food the animals didn't eat. This was heartbreaking, to say the least. The kids in this area were pretty much homeless. Their parents had either died from drug overdoses, gun violence, or the AIDs virus. It was really sad. Of course I would pray for them, give them food, and let them know I came from the gutter too. I told them about King Jesus and how he could transform their lives. It was clear to me how much work needed to be done in Juarez for Gods glory.

These kids actually lived in pallet houses made out of wood and cardboard. The area they lived in looks like a dump site where you would throw trash away. There was no electricity and no water. I could never understand why many of my preacher friends didn't want to go help out and preach and bring hope to Juarez.

My preacher connections thought I was crazy. I'd ask them, "Where do you think Jesus would be preaching if he was on earth right now? Do you think he would only be preaching at big nice church buildings, or do you think he would be preaching somewhere equivalent to Jerusalem? Back in his days, He would definitely be preaching in Juarez, Mexico, one of the most dangerous places on earth that need God's Word, hope, and salvation. Don't you have Jesus living inside of you? Aren't you the salt and light of the world?"

I always try to make them think. I know everyone is not like me and I know they're scared to go, but if we don't do it, who will? I'm pretty sure everyone in the Bible did not want to go to many of the places they did and risk their lives, but *There Is a Cause*, and we as believers have to let it be known we come with power also, and our power and boldness comes from above. It comes from God Almighty and God's riding with us just as he did with the Apostle Paul and the disciples.

Around this time my homeboy Fish had gotten out of prison and he had been deported to Juarez. Many of my homeboys had. I was excited to see him. It had been around sixteen years since I had gotten a chance to kick it with him. He'd been locked up non-stop.

I went to Juarez to visit him. My little sister went to see Fish a week before me. She told me he had asked her, "Where's my carnal Huero?" She told him I was sick with a really bad cough or I'd have come.

She told me he immediately made a guy that was there with him get me penicillin. This homeboy he was with said all the pharmacies were closed.  Fish made him get me some anyway. When this guy got back, he handed it to her like it was drugs. He whispered to her, "Here's your carnal's medication. If he needs anything from Juarez, tell him to just send the word and we will make sure he gets it."

When she told me this, I started laughing, but I took the medication Fish sent me. I was better within a week then I went to see him. I told him to meet me at a restaurant. My cousin gave him a ride and I arrived in my ride. When we both got out of the cars I said, "Orale que rollo, Fish," and he said "Que rollo Huero." We gave each other a big hug. Then he said, "Man Huero, you look old."

I told him the same. "We're getting older, carnal." It was good to see him. He had tattoos everywhere - his neck, his arms, chest and back were covered.

"Man, Fish, you look like a chalkboard written on with no more room to write on."

We both laughed. I'd picked the restaurant because it was a really upper-class seafood restaurant in Mexico. We were both really happy to see each other. We both joked and laughed. I asked him what he wanted to eat.

"I don't know, Huero. I've never been to a restaurant this nice. I've been locked up my whole life. You know that."

I suggested the lobster and crab. "You'll like it." I was thankful to God that I was able to be a blessing to my friend who really was like a

brother to me. I shared Jesus with him, of
course, letting him know how good God had been to me.

He listened to me and I know it touched him because he knew me.
He knew how I used to be. The truth was that I used to be worse than Fish.
I had just stopped living the lifestyle and he didn't. He went into it full
force.

Many, if not everyone, would look at my homeboy Fish like he
was a killer and be really scared of him. I didn't see him that way. God
had given me a grace towards people like Fish. I understood where they
were coming from because I was the same way. The only difference
between me and Fish is I found Jesus. I never looked down on people like
Fish because without God I would be the same or worse.

After we ate, I wanted to do something nice for Fish. We went to a
clothing store and I bought him socks, boxers, pants and a jacket. The
whole time I was talking and bragging about God.

My cousin that gave Fish the ride that day later told me that Fish
said, "Man, Huero's really changed a lot, hasn't he?"

She'd said, "Yeah, he's definitely not the same person he used to
be."

After shopping for Fish, I got us a really nice hotel. We stayed up
all night. He played around on a chair like a kid, and then he stopped and
said, "Sorry Huero."

I said, "No need to apologize. Feel free to be yourself." It hit me
that he was joking and playing around because he never had a childhood.
He always had to act hard and be hard, doing all the time he had done. I
understood this because I used to have to put on a front when I was doing
time and lived like that.

I talked about all the places and cities I had been to preaching the
gospel. To my amazement Fish had been to many of the states and cities
too. I asked him how.

"I've traveled the country in chains, doing time everywhere."

It tripped me out.

Fish kept admiring my gold chain necklace. I took it off and gave it
to him. He didn't want to take it, but I insisted. I told him to just take care
of it.

I kept telling him about Jesus. He started telling me everything criminal he was involved in in Mexico.

"Fish, stop doing what you're doing. God stands against what you're doing. You need to change."

My cousin later told me that Fish saw me preaching on TV. She said he was so excited, telling all the homeboys he was with, "Shut up! My homeboy's preaching on TV." She said he raised the volume high on the TV, and while everyone else was partying, he was listening to me preach. I was talking about how I grew up.

My cousin said when I started talking about how my homeboys grew up and lived, he was pointing at himself, saying, "That's me. Huero's talking about me."

It made me laugh. I told her that was cool and to tell him I send my love and that Jesus loves him too.

She never got that chance. The next thing I knew, Fish was on worldwide TV for all types of charges in Mexico. My homeboy Fish couldn't even stay free in Mexico where the law was corrupt and way more lenient. The next time I saw him was in a Mexican prison. Fish is still locked up to this very day.

When I went to visit him in prison, I went in as a preacher. I had to talk to the warden. I told her I wanted to preach to the worst of the worst inmates. She looked at me like I was crazy and she said, "Let me see your preaching papers, your documentation."

I showed her many different things proving I really preached the gospel. After this, she said, "Look, I don't mind you preaching to these guys. They need the inspiration, but maybe you should start by preaching to normal inmates who aren't so dangerous."

The reason I wanted to preach to the worst of the worst is that I knew Fish was there. I told the warden, "I'm not scared to die preaching the gospel of Jesus Christ, and I want to preach to the very worst." She granted me access.

Fish was in one of the worst, most violent maximum security prisons in Mexico. When I got to the area Fish was in, the guards asked me, "Who do you want to preach to?" I gave them Fish's real name and told them his mom wanted me to preach to him, which was really the truth.

I waited in a room where the glass between prisoners and visitors was at least six inches thick. There were no speakers or holes in the window to speak through.

When Fish came out, the guards had him chained and walked him in with guns on them, ready to shoot him if he tried to do anything stupid. They had masks covering their faces.

Fish looked straight down at the floor. When the guard left, he looked up and said, "Que rollo, Huero, how you been?"

"Good, Fish, how you been?"

He said he was OK.

"Why were you looking down? Why didn't you look at the guards?"

"I can't. I'm considered an enemy of the country. If I even look up they will beat me until I'm almost dead."

"Man, that's messed up. How are the conditions here?"

"Horrible. They haven't been feeding me and I've been locked down in a room hardcore."

"It can't be worse than America lockdown, right?"

"Huero, I wish I was locked up over there. They've been torturing me hardcore, every three days, trying to get me to talk and give them any type of information they can get. But guess what? I haven't said a word. I ain't no rat. You already know how we get down in Big Bad Jackie's gang, Huero."

I thought to myself, "My homeboy Fish is as down as they come. He just needs to turn that negative energy into positive energy for Christ."

Fish said, "Hey, Huero thanks for coming to visit me, carnal. You are my true brother and I appreciate it. You are my closest homeboy. We are family. I love you, all the homeboys love you. Everyone knows you've changed and are down for God now. Everyone respects you, even my mom. She always tells me how bad Huero was, and if he changed, I can change. You give us all hope, me and all the homeboys, because you let us know change is possible. My mom gets hope from you, knowing one day I can change. I know you, Huero, and if you hadn't changed and found God, you would be locked up right next to me, riding with me."

"Fish, I believe you're still alive because of my prayers. I believe God has such a beautiful plan for your life just like he did for mine. I love you and God loves you, and one day you will be a soldier for Christ with one amazing testimony. People probably look at you like you're the worst of the worst, but God looks at you through the eyes of Jesus, and Fish, there is always hope in Jesus. Get a hold of a Bible and start reading it, because it's God's guide to truth and life. I'll always be your homeboy and I'll always be praying for your salvation."

I said goodbye to my childhood friend that day and left, asking God to have mercy on him. I prayed, "I know his heart, and he does have a good heart, he just needs you, Jesus. He needs your unconditional love."

Every time I saw any of my homeboys, it broke my heart because I knew if they would only accept Jesus Christ as their Lord and Savior, their spiritual eyes would open as they got closer to God's heart.

46.

## Crazy White Lady

I started getting invited to preach all over the place. I'd been invited as a special guest to speak to ministers and leaders in Tennessee.  I could've gone to California and I really wanted to go, but for some reason I felt God wanted me to go to Tennessee. I listened to God and went to Tennessee. I'm sure glad I did because I met someone who was a fellow minister of the gospel who would be one of my all-time favorite connections in God's kingdom.

When I got there, I was being my normal jokester self with all the preachers that were there. I preached to everyone the first night. Everyone loved it because I was such a different type of preacher.

The next night I heard this white lady preach, and she was a fire preacher. She got so riled up that she was actually turning red and hopping up and down.

I couldn't help it. I started laughing.

She had short hair and she turned red as she hopped up and down. She looked like a chicken, but my laughter soon turned. She was hardcore and no joke. I knew then why God had me go to Tennessee. It was to meet a great person and friend named Gale Dalton from Ohio. After she preached, we started talking. She hadn't wanted to come to Tennessee either, but she also felt God wanted her to come, so she did. When she heard me preach she said the same thing.  She was there to meet and connect with me.

I invited her to preach in El Paso and Juarez, and New Mexico whenever she wanted.

When I got back to El Paso and Gale called me about a week later and said, "I'm ready to go preach for you and people you know when you're ready."

"I'm ready for you to come out, but Gale, I will tell you this: I'll hook you up at some nice churches but I'm also taking you to areas where the devil, our enemy, has strongholds from the Mexican prisons to the streets in Mexico."

I always say this to test preacher's hearts, and without hesitating she responded, "Let's do this. When I wake up, the devil hears my armor clank. He knows a warrior for God has her feet on the ground that ain't scared to die."

I loved it. God was answering my prayers of hooking me up with other hardcore believers, other radicals for Christ who thought just like me. I was excited to see what God was going to do when Gale came out, and boy, it was going to be amazing.

When she got to El Paso, she came with three other women from her ministry. I'd set her up to preach ten straight days. The first day she was preaching in the Segundo Barrio area in El Paso, one of my old stomping grounds, with a good friend and well known pastor. When she preached there, my pastor friend and I were laughing because she was preaching like a maniac, jumping on all the church chairs and running around the church building. Everyone loved her.

The second place I had her preach at was a mega church in Juarez, but before she preached I asked my pastor friend to show her the area where kids lived, the one that looked like a dump site where they lived in pallet houses and ate leftover pig and cow food. It's something I always did, and still do to this very day, to all who come preach for me. I want them to understand the need where I preach.

The year was 2008 when the Juarez violence was at an all-time high. The murder rate was crazy, and at that time Juarez was considered the most dangerous place on earth. Everyone thought I was crazy for preaching in Juarez. I can imagine what they thought about Gale going over there to preach.

It was a great time to be preaching in Juarez. The fact is you could die.

I have pictures of many other preachers who were hardcore like me that died preaching the gospel. But to me it was exciting, knowing I was hitting the devil where it hurts, and that I was doing some hardcore ministry like I read in the Bible.

When Gale and her guests saw this, they broke down crying. It was a horrible thing to see.

I told her, "That's why I wanted you to come. They need more people shining the light of Jesus. They need some real hope besides seeing all the negativity that's around them 24/7."

After Gale finished preaching, hundreds of people came up for prayer. She prayed for every single one of them.

The third day she preached in a Mexican prison in Juarez to thousands of inmates. Many got saved and prayed for that day. After crossing the border back into El Paso, I took Gale to Segundo Barrio to pray for some of my homeboys. One of them was Koko. After praying for him, I got back into the vehicle. One of the guests that was with Gale started crying, saying, "Pastor Isaiah, you really care for these people don't you?"

"Yes, they're my people, they're God's people. Most people don't care about them, but I do. God blesses me with big connections in God's kingdom ministry wise, but the truth is I don't look for them. Hurt, broke down people is who I look for. I tell them I see them through God's eyes. I see them changed, I feel them changed, and I go towards these hurt people believing that. In doing so, big preachers come looking for me. It's just how God has always worked with me. I understand these broken down people, because I used to live like them. I tell them God's a great God, and His mercy and forgiveness is for everyone."

The fourth day she went to the red light district in Juarez from night to early morning where all the bars, gang violence and prostitution occurred.

One of my pastor friends who was with us told us what not to do before going into the Juarez streets. He told Gale and guests not to get involved if they see illegal activity or if violence occurs. For instance, if someone was getting beat up, stabbed, or killed in the streets, never get involved, because it could be a drug deal gone bad, or someone's sister could have been molested.

He said, "If you were to get involved, it would mean nothing to these types of people to hurt you or even kill you. That's the risk every time you minister in Juarez."

Again, to me it was very worth the risk for spreading and preaching the gospel to lost souls.

One time, some ministers took a picture of a taco stand because they wanted a photo of the man serving tacos. What they didn't know was someone was doing a drug deal right next to the taco stand. These guys thought they were law enforcement and were going to kill them. My friend had to explain to them that they were preachers taking a picture of a taco stand.

Most the time, mafia members will be watching you with binoculars when you're crossing the bridge from America to Mexico. They observe what kind of car you drive, whether it looks expensive. Even if you're walking across, they're looking to see if it looks like you have money. You can become a target without even knowing it. It's always good to go with someone who knows these things.

After the talk, Gale agreed that we hit the streets. As soon as we walked out of the church doors, not even a half a block away, guards were chasing an escaped inmate. They caught him and started beating him with flash lights until he was a bloody mess.

This literally happened right in front of my friend Gale. She must have thought, *"OK, this is the real deal."* When it came to preaching, it didn't deter her.

I was being my normal self as always, joking around and laughing. I love preaching in those types of situations. To me it is very exciting, knowing I am being a light for Jesus. None of that is new to me. It's been a part of my lifestyle in the past.

Gale and her team preached to everyone they could, whether prostitutes, gang members, drunks, drug addicts, or homeless people. It was awesome. We had an amazing time and many souls were saved.

The fifth, sixth, and seventh day, I hooked her up at an outreach in downtown El Paso. It was in a poverty stricken project by a big high school.

I announced it when I was preaching on TV, so other pastors and ministries came together with me. The turnout was amazing. The first night there must have been 400 people there. The second night 500, and the third night around 700 attended. We gave out free burgers, hotdogs and drinks.

Everyone was really touched by the event. There were even people sitting on top of the project apartment rooftops, listening as the gospel was preached. Many people got saved and knew who our sweet Jesus was.

One kid that was bald with a ponytail was riding a bicycle. He was probably six or seven years old. All the kids there said, "He needs prayer. He's the worst." He circled with his bike multiple times around the area where we preachers were. He was scoping the scene.

He finally stopped and got off his bike. When he saw Gale pray for people, it intrigued him. He walked up and said, "I want some of that to see if it's true." The kid loved it. He asked if he could have what we have, so we led him to God on the spot.

I hooked her up at three other places within those ten days. Over 800 people accepted Jesus Christ as their Lord and Savior.

My homeboy Manny was sending me letters from prison. He had gotten locked up again. I was always sending him gospel tracts. He really liked one of them, and it was one of my favorites too, because it reminded me of us. It was named 'The Bull' and was about a hardcore guy that no one could reach. He ended up finding Jesus and his life changed.

Manny really liked that tract. I showed his wife and mom the letters he would write to me. They couldn't believe he would write to me about Jesus. His wife was a homegirl from our hood. It brought tears to her eyes.

"Huero, please keep talking to him about God, because he doesn't talk to anyone like that. You're reaching him."

It brought joy to my heart.

Gale asked me to go to Ohio to preach for her. The next thing I knew I was headed to Ohio to preach the gospel.

When I got there I met Gale's husband, who like me, had lived crazy. He was an old school gangster, but a white one. We really got along because we both served Jesus now, and in our old life we had both done time behind bars. Gale and her husband Denny were family to me, as close as blood. They took me up to see their church. It's a very beautiful church. Pastor Denny told me how he had sold some cars he had to put funds into the building program. They have a 50 acre property with ponds and all. They were like me. They dreamed big for Jesus.

It doesn't mean we don't have problems and issues in life. We just choose not to look at the temporary; we see the future through our spiritual eyes. We are not seeing through carnal eyes.

We had a lot in common even though our environments where we grew up were totally different.

It was very quiet at their property, so quiet that you could hear crickets, which for a city boy was not normal at all. You could hear frogs on their ponds, deer would pass by you and it was very green with trees everywhere.

I think it was a culture shock for Gale when coming to El Paso and Juarez. In El Paso you're lucky, or have to work hard to even have green grass.

Gale and Denny said, "We made a video of us preaching together in El Paso and Juarez with all the pictures we took." They put the video on. There were other people with us watching it too. When the video came on, Juarez looked like a war zone compared to where they were from. I remember tears running down everyone's faces when the video was playing. This is the first time I really understood how unique my ministry was.

God started speaking to me saying, "Your ministry and the areas you preach in might be normal to you but it's not normal to everyone else."

I was in their beautiful house looking out the window at all the greenery and beautiful trees. It really hit me hard. I thanked God for using me and connecting me to amazing men and women of God.

When I preached for them, the people loved me because I was such a different type of preacher. It was how the people felt having Gale in our area. The people in Juarez nicknamed Gale 'the crazy white lady.' It was funny.

47.

## Changes and a Vision

When I got back to El Paso, my wife and I were not on good terms and I could feel something was not right. I remember getting into the car with her one day and I could smell a
horrible smell. The stench was really strong. I knew God was trying to show me something.

I asked her why it smelled so bad.

"What are you talking about? I have perfume on."

"It's not a physical smell. God is showing me something in the spiritual realm. What are you doing wrong? Something's wrong."

She looked at me and said nothing, but I knew without a doubt that God was showing me something was not right.

Months passed as I prayed to God to either change her heart or let her leave me if she's never gonna really change, even if it hurt me because of my kids. I loved my kids with all my heart and I never wanted them to feel as if I wouldn't be there for them. I believe God heard my prayer because she was really on the wrong track. I was about to find out how much the devil was influencing her and her mindset. She was lost, and what was gonna happen next I wouldn't have believed if it was not for God giving me insight and nudging me in my spirit.

I started catching her in many lies. The next thing I knew she was leaving me. I told her, "I really hope this is what you want, because if you leave I'm going on with my life." She laughed in my face and left.

I wasn't really happy either. It was more about my kids. I lost everything, including my beautiful home, and ended up at my little sister's trailer in an extra room she had which was a little bit bigger than a lock down cell in a facility.

I couldn't sleep for three days in that little room. I prayed on my knees asking God why this was happening to me.

The third day God spoke to me and said, "Do you think I'm worried about you?"

"No, God."

"Why?"

"Because worrying is a sin and you're God."

"Then why are you worrying if you're my son?" He then proceeded to ask me questions. He asked, and really told me at the same time, "You said even if you lost everything you would serve me. Is that still true?"

"Yes, God."

"Even if you were in prison you would preach for me? Is that still true?"

"Yes, God."

"You said you would even risk your life even if it meant death. Is that still true?"

"God, I go to Juarez and risk my life all the time. You know I'm living this."

"Then what are we gonna do?"

I responded, "Let's keep this rolling, God. Let's keep hitting this stupid devil."

That night I slept but I got woken up by an amazing vision God gave me. In the vision I was dressed in a robe of righteousness. I had a crown on my head and God was in front of me. I couldn't see his face because it was shining so bright and his robe was full of diamonds. It shone sparkling bright. He had a big crown on his head. God and I both had swords, and God swung his sword at me and I swung my sword back at him. After a few times doing this with the swords, I told God, "I don't want to fight against you. I stand with you." Now what's crazy is when me and God spoke to each other in the vision, we did so without opening our mouths. We would talk with our minds and we could understand each other completely. The last time God swung His sword as I swung mine, I said again, "God, I don't want to fight with you."

God spoke and said, "I'm not fighting with you, I am training you personally to rise up an army from where you come from," meaning people who still lived the lifestyle I used to. I woke up sweating, amazed and tripping out about the vision I'd just had.

My grandpa on my dad's side, and so-called Christian friends, were acting as if it was my fault that everything had gone wrong with me and my wife. I am not perfect. If any preacher is a 100 percent honest in telling you that, it would be me.

Even wife's cousin told me, "This happened because you put God ahead of everything in your life. Look at me. Me and my wife party and do drugs together and are happy."

"Yeah, I put God first, and he will always come first in my life. I would rather be in a cell for the rest of my life than live in the world and go to hell. It doesn't matter who stands for God with me, even if no one does, I'm still gonna serve God."

I started praying. I asked God if it really was my fault, then to bring light on what I did wrong, but if it's her fault, bring it into the light for all to see.

God answered my prayer. I found out she was cheating on me but not with a man. She was cheating on me with a woman. I was glad the truth finally came to light. All the people who accused me looked ignorant when the truth was revealed. I made mistakes, I know that, but I was not doing everything my wife was doing.

The Bible says to be equally yoked when you're married, and the truth was we had not been equally yoked - ever. We were two screwed up kids who never had a chance without God first in our lives.

So I filed for divorce and got joint custody of our children.

It was time for a fresh start.

48.

Beautiful

One day going home to my sister's, and not by coincidence, my old homeboy who used to sell large amounts of cocaine with, was right across the street. As I pulled up to park my vehicle, he waved me down.

"What's up, Huero? What you doing homie? How you been?"

I said, "Good, just getting to my sister's."

He said, "I heard you had a business and lived in a big nice house."

"Not no more. Me and my wife divorced."

"Why don't you roll with me tonight?"

"Nah, carnal. I don't do that no more."

He looked me in my eyes and said, "I heard you've been preaching now."

"I am. I love Jesus Christ with all my heart."

He really tripped out. "I heard that, but I never believed it. It's like I'm looking at the old Huero, but it's not you anymore."

"I'm not the old Huero. I'm a redeemed Huero now, full of God's grace."

Man! He tripped out. "Look, Huero, what if I give you a kilo, free, to start riding with me again?"

"No thanks. God bless you. I'll be praying for you."

When I was talking with him, I could feel pure evil. It was crazy to me, because before I would get so crazy and rowdy with him at bars that he would actually tell me, "Hey Huero, be cool. Stop tripping out wanting to stab everyone." God had changed me and my heart so much. I was nowhere near how I used to be.

When I got to my little room at my sister's I started praying, asking God to keep my mind focused on the gospel. I couldn't believe how the devil operates and comes and offers you a kilo through people I once was close to. He is a deceiver and a liar. I wanted no part of that life ever again, and at that time in my life I needed money bad, and a kilo was worth more than $25,000 at the time. I recognized the devil's lie.

I was really concerned about my kids, and I knew I had to be the same dad, full of God and faith for them.

Many women called me from churches all over where I'd preached. They would say God told them we were meant to be together to preach the gospel. I wasn't looking for a woman at the time. I really didn't care about that. I was more concerned about my kids and my ministry than anything else.

Six months passed and Gale wanted to come back to preach and I said let's do it. I needed to do some hardcore ministry with someone I considered family. When I bring special guest preachers out, I always give good offerings and hotels. It's something I learned from my pastor Joshua Krishna.

By the way, Pastor Krishna stood by me through everything I was going through, always uplifting my faith. I was very thankful for him. It's good to know someone is praying
for you and on your side. I will always honor him. He's been the best mentor I could've ever asked for. My heart is forever grateful towards him for all he's done for me.

Gale coming out was what I needed. When she got to El Paso and Juarez we had amazing services again with many souls saved. After I gave her an offering, I had like $450 left to my name, but it didn't matter to me. The truth is I would have given her every penny I had. I love Gale, so it was nothing to do so.

Before she left, I told her what had happened between me and my ex. She told me I should talk to her niece Evelyn, who was going through the same thing. Evelyn's ex-husband was beating her and treating her horrible.

I had met Evelyn when I preached in Ohio, and there was no question that her heart was God's heart. She loved Jesus will all her mind, body, and soul. I figured it would be OK to talk to her about issues we were both dealing with. Plus, I considered her a friend and thought to myself, *"She's all the way in Ohio and I'm in El Paso. That would be cool."*

I used to ask myself how preachers got divorced. I could never understand it until it happened to me.

Evelyn and I ended up talking, and it was great because we both loved God and could talk to one another about what we were going through. We first started talking every few days, and then we started talking on a daily basis. Months passed and we became good friends.

We were talking on the phone as usual and I was sharing a new sermon I was working on. She asked me if I liked her and I said "Sure I do, I love you, sister."

She said, "Don't give me that 'sister' stuff. Do you like me?"

I said, "Yes, of course."

"Look, you got to stop beating around the bush, because I'm falling in love with you."

This really scared me, but the truth was I really liked her too, but I wanted to take things as slow as possible. I didn't want to rush into anything.

After another year she was asking me, "When are you gonna marry me?"

I would say, "Give me two years."

She'd get mad. "What am I? A prison sentence?"

I would laugh. I was really planning on waiting five to seven years. I just wouldn't tell her that. We had seen each other a few times with Gale and preaching since we had been talking, but we had never been totally alone.

I was talking to my homeboy Valdo and a few others about Evelyn, telling them how beautiful she was and how much she loved God. They asked me if we had fooled around and I said no. They asked me, "What if she makes the moves on you?"

"Can't do it man."

They'd crack up at me, laughing so hard their stomachs hurt. "That's not the Huero we know."

"You guys can laugh all you want, but I'm gonna do it God's way this time. When has anything gone right doing it our way? We've been with girls without being married and putting God first and our relationships have failed."

They stopped laughing and said, "You're right, Huero, it just is funny hearing you say that, knowing how you used to be."

I said, "Yeah man. I'm gonna do it God's way."

Things were going really good for me again. I'd moved into a two-bedroom condo apartment and I loved the peace of living alone. My kids would come over a lot too, so it was cool. I enjoyed it to the fullest.

I was planning to bring Evelyn out and drive her to California and propose to her because I did love her very much. I didn't tell her I was going to propose, but I thought it would make her happy. I told her, "Look beautiful, I'm gonna fly you out to El Paso, then we're going to California. I want to do something special for you."

"Do you want to get married when I get there?"

"No."

I'd bought a ring for the proposal. She talked to Gale and Gale told her, "God told me when you get there, you're getting married, so be ready."

Evelyn told me what Gale said, but I said, "No, we're not getting married yet."

She started praying. Later, she told me her prayer. "God, everyone either looks up to Isaiah or is his friend. There are very few he allows to speak into his life, so I'm asking you to have someone he looks up to speak to him about marrying me."

Wouldn't you know it? My mentor, Pastor Joshua Krishna called me. I answered by saying, "What up, PK?"

He immediately started going off on me saying, "What's going on with this girl you've been dating?"

"Nothing, PK."

"Don't you lie to me. Isaiah, I'm in your life because I love you. Other people might want things from you. I don't. I'm working with you because you need a mentor in your life. It's a God thing. I love you and want nothing but to see you succeed in your God-given gifts. Do you love this girl?"

"Yeah, I guess."

"What's that supposed to mean, 'I guess?' Do you love her or not?"

"Yeah, PK, I do."

"Have you messed around with her yet?"

"No, not yet."

He got mad and said, "What does that mean, not yet?"

"I'm gonna drive with her to California and propose to her out there. I wanted her to meet you."

"You, her, and who else?"

"Just me and her."

"Come on, Isaiah. I know you. You're a man's man. Do you believe you are gonna come drive all the way out here and you're not gonna do something stupid?"

I really had not thought that through. We had always been around other preachers when together.

"Are you in love with this girl because of her looks or because of the God in her? Do you really want to be with her for the rest of your life?"

"Yes, PK, I do want to be with her."

"Man up and do the right thing. We both know you cannot afford another divorce."

"PK, then you think I should marry her?"

He yelled, "Either marry her or leave the girl alone!" He hung up on me.

I called Evelyn immediately and said, "My mentor called me and seemed to be really mad. Do you think I'm doing something wrong? He rarely calls me like that. If he does, I know it's for my good."

"What did he say?"

I told her and she said, "God heard my prayer."

"Yes, He surely did. As soon as you get here, we're getting married."

She said, "Pastor Krishna is a man of God. He listened to God and told you what I asked God to tell you through someone you would listen to."

Evelyn got to El Paso. I had the wedding ring tied to roses on a ribbon sitting on the passenger seat in my vehicle. She wouldn't see the wedding ring unless she really looked hard, trying to find it. I did that on purpose.

I went into the airport waiting on my beautiful wife-to-be. We ate in the airport. When we got to my vehicle, I opened her door.

"What's that on the seat?" She picked up the roses and smelled them and said, "They're beautiful."

"What's that hanging on the ribbon?"

She looked at the ribbon and saw the white gold diamond ring.

I got down on my knee and said, "Beautiful, you are the best thing that has ever happened to me. I love you and you own my heart."

I said many other things and asked her to marry me. She cried, and agreed, and we went to the courthouse and were married.

We went to California to celebrate our honeymoon. We stopped in Arizona to relax. When we got our luggage into our hotel room, my homeboy Valdo called me.

"I got married today." I was very happy.

He said, "Congratulations."

"Thanks, carnal."

"I'm sorry to tell you this, but my brother Manny is dead."

"What do you mean?"

"Yeah, Huero, he's dead."

We hung up. I couldn't believe it. I had just talked to him a few weeks earlier. I've had many friends die, but none of them had the effect the death of my homeboy Manny had on me. I still think about him. He'd called me just weeks earlier.

"I'm free. I got out of prison, carnal." He spoke to me in Spanish and said, "I just called to say thank you for always writing to me and sending me Godly tracts and money."

"Don't worry about it. That was God just working through me."

His voice started to break down. He was so touched, he was starting to cry.

"Jesus loves you, Manny, and he has great plans for your life. You're going to be a testimony for Christ, as I am."

I was sitting on the edge of our bed in our hotel and Evelyn asked me what was wrong. I was quiet, just thinking about my homeboy that just died. I told her about it, and she hugged me saying, "I'm so sorry."

I said, "It's just crazy. I've lost so many homeboys I grew up with. I hate to say this, but it's normal where I come from. I really hope Manny had the chance to get right with Jesus before he died."

I really miss my homeboy Manny. I think about him all the time.

We got to California and stopped in Southern California first. We had a blast. We rode a jet ski together, which was fun. I'm terrified of sharks, especially great white sharks and California has many, but I got out there on the water anyway. We were eating at a restaurant on the ocean and the people riding them looked like they were having so much fun.

Spontaneous me said, "Get up, let's go."

Evelyn said, "Where?"

"Jet skiing."

We got into wetsuits and off we went into the deep ocean. This was crazy for me because I had never gone in further than my ankles. Most friends would laugh at me and tell me to go all the way in. I would tell them, "No way, I'm not gonna be one of those guys on the news without a leg, saying a shark bit my leg off. I would rather be in a jailhouse riot than be in the ocean with a great white shark." I was not lying either.

I drove the Jet Ski with Evelyn on my back, her arms around me. I told her, "I'm scared of sharks."

It was so deep I freaked out and started driving full throttle. We were hitting big waves and flying in the air. She was telling me to slow down.

"No way." But then I did because I saw dolphins and I knew from watching TV that dolphins didn't like sharks. I stopped and three dolphins started circling around our jet ski. They were so close to us, we could touch them. It was amazing. We were both saying to each other how amazing God is.

I also took her to Disneyland and Universal Studios for her first time. We did many other things and were off to San Francisco so my beautiful wife could meet Pastor Krishna.

He took us to a really nice restaurant right on the ocean and then he got right down to business. He asked Evelyn her name, then said, "Before we order, answer this: what is the greatest quality you see in one another? Go," then he pointed to Evelyn. After she answered he pointed at me and I answered.

"Good, those are really good answers." Pastor Krishna is like that - blunt, to the point, and real. It's something I really love about him. He always shoots me straight.

Evelyn started telling him she knew he was a man of God because he had called me and heard God's voice about what she had prayed, and how she told God to let me have it from someone I listened to.

He said, "Oh, Isaiah listens to me. He'd better."

I laughed because it was the truth.

I offered to pay the bill for lunch, but he insisted. I asked again, and Evelyn said, "He always tries to pay all preachers' lunch bills. He doesn't listen and let them pay once in a while."

Pastor said, "I'm paying, that's all there is to it. Isaiah, be quiet and listen."

"OK, PK."

Evelyn laughed and said, "That's something I've never seen."

Pastor Krishna said, "If Isaiah ever gives you trouble, you call me and let me know and I'll handle him."

She said, Thank you, Pastor Krishna," and until this very day, if I'm not listening to her, she threatens me with calling Pastor Krishna.

I always respond, "I will deny all allegations."

Pastor Krishna liked Evelyn, which to me was really important.

49.

Ready to Launch

After we left California we went to Dallas, Texas to my cousin's. My aunt had made us a beautiful wedding cake with chocolate strawberries. It was pretty cool of them.

Then Evelyn went back to Ohio and I went home to El Paso to get a house for us. Evelyn was leaving Ohio to move with me. She left everything she knew; her family, friends, and Gale to be with me. It showed me how in love she was with me. I appreciate that there's not many that would leave everything they know for their spouse.

I got us a newly built, three-bedroom house. Before I got the house, she asked me how I was going to get it.

"Easy. It's like buying a car. Once you've bought one, you know it's possible to get another one." It's a principal God showed me. "Once you've done something, and God has blessed you to do it once, you know God can do it again. Nothing can stop you when this type of revelation is revealed to you."

I've always said the devil can't stop anything God has planned for you. He can prolong it, but he can't stop it, especially when you already know it's possible.

Evelyn went from being in Gale's ministry to being in mine, and boy, we are a great team. I preach, and then my wife prays for people, and when she does, God moves in a mighty way. It was always what I desired for my ministry.

Evelyn got a taste of how much I preached when we went on my east coast preaching tour, as I call it. Our first stop was Chicago.

I preached the morning we got there at one church then we went to preach at another church in Chicago at night time. After that we drove to Michigan. We got there at 3:00 a.m. and woke up to preach at 8:00 a.m., then I preached again at night, went to fellowship afterwards to eat, as I usually do with my pastor friends I preach for, then we were off to Indianapolis, Indiana.

We got to our hotel around 3:00 a.m. again. I remember walking into our hotel with our luggage. I turned around and looked at Beautiful, which is what I call my wife Evelyn to this very day. A lot of places I preach call her 'Beautiful' when they talk to her because they don't know her name. I turned to her and she looked drained. I asked her if she was feeling alright she replied, "Yeah, I'm a little tired, but I love preaching God's Word and that I can do this with you. I was proud to have a wife that understood that there was a cause that we stood for bigger than ourselves now.

Many say I'm like a racehorse that never stops, and I am, I know. It's very important that this gospel is preached to as many people as I possibly can preach it to. I think many times people hearing me preach think, "Man, this guy goes everywhere preaching and gets to travel everywhere and go sightseeing." That's simply not true. A lot of times I'm so busy preaching and going to different cities, states, and countries that I don't even get good sleep or rest. Don't get me wrong. It is the best. I love preaching the gospel and I'm honored to do so. I always will until the day I die.

I preached in Indianapolis, and then we went to Lafayette, Indiana with a pastor I had met through a friend in Chicago. When I met this pastor, who now is a good friend of mine, I went to his house because my friend from Chicago wanted me to visit him. He said God wanted me to meet him.

I was exhausted. I didn't want to stop and meet him. I had preached locally in El Paso and then I got on a flight and preached in Ohio, then in Indiana. I was supposed to preach the next morning in Chicago. I was only going to get three hours of sleep before preaching, but my friend wanted me to meet this other pastor. Until this day he laughs about me not wanting to meet him because he does big things for God and people in his church literally wait up to two months to schedule an appointment with him. I didn't know this at the time. When I finally met him he was awesome. I was glad my friend had taken me to meet him. He actually preaches around the world.

When I met him at his house, he told me, "I'm gonna be traveling through El Paso. When I do, I'm gonna meet up with you." This has become a tradition for us. If I'm in his area, I always preach for him and if he's in my area we always meet up, he always makes time for me. It's really favor that God has placed on my life with all my connections.

This was the first time I was gonna preach for him in Lafayette. I really didn't know if it was a small church or big church, and really I didn't care. He knew all about me from his visits to El Paso, and he was excited to have me preaching for him.

When I got there it really tripped my wife out. She asked if this was the church and I said, "Yes, Beautiful, it is." It was a mega church that had thousands of members. I think the building is worth like 30 or 40 million. When we walked in it was crazy.

Years ago God told me I was going to preach at places like these. It was amazing. This church even has elevators. It is very beautiful. As we checked out their book store and then walked into one of the entrances into the sanctuary, the ushers opened the door for me and said, "You must be Pastor Isaiah Blancas."

"I am."

"We've heard so much about you. We are all excited to hear you preach. It's great to put a face to the name."

"Well, thank you."

Beautiful asked me what I was thinking. "Are you nervous? Are you freaking out? What are you feeling?"

The truth was that I was in a zone. "Beautiful, I'm excited. I was meant for this, to preach the gospel."

I think the crowd tripped out on me because of how real I was in my sermon. I told them, "I've got to be honest with you all. I would rather be preaching in the streets to prostitutes and gang members than to you guys, because they need Jesus. You guys know Jesus, they don't. I'm not saying I'm not happy to be here because I am, but I'm just being real with you guys."

The people loved me. My pastor friend asked if they wanted prayer from me and a line formed of around 200 people. The way my wife and I operate is that I preach and she prays. If we roll solo, then we preach and pray by ourselves. This was not the case on this day. Beautiful looked up at me and pretty much said with her eyes and gestures, "Don't even try to call me up for this big line of people by myself."

I said to the 200 plus line, "The way my wife, Beautiful, and I work as a ministry is I'll preach and she prays." I reassured them God moves through her in an amazing way. I called her up and sat down. I was laughing as I did. To this day she gets mad about it in a joking way. I even took pictures when she was praying for all the people. Once in a while I'll still show the pictures to her to mess with her.

Around this time Pastor Krishna ordained me. I had been ordained in El Paso years before but I was beyond happy to get my ordination papers from my pastor. I keep them in my room on a shelf. It's a reminder to me of just how far my amazing God has brought me.

Months later I was on my way to meet Pastor Krishna in San Francisco. Evelyn and I met him at a restaurant. He wanted to take us to one that was on a cliff over the Pacific Ocean. It was really cool. I love California and I would preach all over the state, but it hadn't happened much. I often prayed and asked God to open doors for me to preach in California, both north and south.

Pastor Krishna asked me about everywhere I'd been preaching, how Evelyn and I were doing, how my God walk was, how much my bills were, and how I was doing in life in general. I wondered why he was asking me all these questions. Evelyn got up to go use the restroom during our conversation. While she was gone, Pastor Krishna said to me, "You're ready, Isaiah."

"Ready for what?"

"You're ready to preach with the big boys. You're going to be preaching for me once a year from now on, and I'm gonna treat you like I treat all of my guest speakers. I'm gonna get hotels for you and take you out to really nice restaurants. When you're my guest you're gonna get a great offering. How does that sound?"

I said, "That sounds good, PK." I was playing it cool but deep down inside I wanted to jump out of my chair and yell, "Yes! I'm gonna preach for my mentor and get treated like royalty. You have to understand. Pastor Krishna has amazing speakers at his church, so to know I was going to be preaching at Embassy and stand on the same pulpit where many greats in God's kingdom stand and preach was such an amazing honor.

After we ate, I told Evelyn what Pastor Krishna said. She was amazed. She said, "Man, I feel like I'm married to someone famous."

I laughed when she said that, but I have to admit it was pretty cool. Remember years and years ago before Pastor Krishna had even ordained me or mentored me, God told me I was going to preach there. I just didn't think it was going to take so long, but that's how my mentor Pastor Krishna rolls. He checks and inspects your fruit before he will even consider you preaching for him. He's a fruit inspector and since I'm his protégé, I think my strong points had to outweigh my flaws, which are many. I guess he had made that decision because he saw growth in my God walk. He saw I was solid; that I was standing on Christ's foundation and wasn't getting off of that foundation, no matter what happened in my life.

One thing I did know was I had to tone my craft. I knew who preached from his pulpit, and I had to bring it at a whole other level. Pastor Krishna had been mentoring me around eight or nine years straight. That's how long it took for him to allow me to preach for him. It didn't happen overnight and I have to admit that I do extra studying on my sermons before I preach for him.

Beautiful says it's the only place I get nervous to preach, but she says, "Since you don't understand what nervous feels like, you can't tell."

But I can now say since he's worked with me and always did things for my good, loved me through all my flaws, I want him to be proud of me when I preach. I am his fruit. I always want him to see spiritual growth in me even though I'm a flawed human being. We are all flawed human beings, only Jesus is perfect and He is my Lord whom I follow after.

When we got back to our home in El Paso, Chaplain Gina's son Tony, who became a friend of mine, came over and said, "You need to meet this ministry of men in Southern California."

He explained how amazing this ministry was in Los Angeles, how a bunch of men got together to praise Jesus and release and share personal things that men deal with no condemnation. He described a judge free zone where men showed grace to one another instead of criticizing one another. He wanted me to visit there, and felt I'd end up preaching there.

I have to be honest. I'm usually nice about it when anyone invites me somewhere, but I usually don't ever go or give it a second thought. The way I meet fellow preachers is usually through connections I already have, or at conferences, but every once and a rare while God speaks to me and tells me I need to go. That's exactly what happened when Tony was telling me about this ministry. I felt God's presence and heard His voice. I drove out the very next week to preach in San Francisco, so I knew I had to stop in LA as God had directed me to.

I called Tony and said, "I'm here. Let's go to this men's ministry." He said, OK, I'll pick you up at your hotel at 6:00 a.m. sharp. "What? 6 a.m.?"

"Yeah, they meet every Saturday at 7 a.m. sharp."

I thought to myself, *"Man these guys must really love God, meeting that early in the morning."* So I went and it was really cool. The guys really liked me and invited me to a house where they were having a ministry party. This is when I would meet another great friend and God connection.

I pulled up to this beautiful house that I found out later was worth millions and millions of dollars. I remember walking into the backyard to the pool area where these guys were having a really big BBQ. There must have been 300 to 500 people there, and the backyard and bar and grill area at this home fit everyone perfectly. They were playing rock-n-roll Christian music with a disco system and live band. You could feel the California vibes in the air. California has always been different from anywhere I had been. They know how to have fun. A lot of these guys were just like me, they were guys that had accepted Jesus, and you could tell a lot of them were street guys just like me. I loved it.

They all had muscle shirts on with their ministry name on them. A whole bunch of them were all tattooed out. The pool area where the band was playing was crazy. It was a tri-level pool with waterfalls. The Jacuzzi was full of people chilling. A volleyball game was going on in the main pool. There were even restrooms outside with showers to wash off if you got dirty for any reason. There were basketball courts on the side of the house, also a little miniature golf course. It was really cool. Steaks and many other food items were coming off the grill.

The guys introduced me to my brotha from another mother, Mr. Vince Garcia. We got acquainted. Almost immediately he said, "You're the Evangelist, aren't you? Go take the microphone away from the singer and preach some. This is my house."

I agreed and introduced myself to everyone and preached for maybe fifteen minutes. He asked me to say some more words around two more times, so I did. The guys liked me, and I liked them too. They were my type of guys, and they gave me a ministry muscle shirt on the spot. I put it on immediately. I understand they usually give the muscle shirts out after a month or so of participation, but they gave me one right away. I still have it.

Vince and I got to spend some time together. I met his wife and kids. They were really good people and they liked us a lot, too. My wife asked Vince, "Hey, brother how'd you get such a beautiful house?"

"Sister, I'm just taking back what the devil has stolen from me with interest."

I use this saying myself. God had me go to connect with my brotha Vince. We talked about doing ministry together and traded phone numbers. I learned that Vince had lived a street life just like me and was actually homeless at thirty-years-old. He's older than me, but we have the same mindset. We both dream big, believing Jesus for the miraculous.

I also found out that movie stars and well-known TV shows on cable, TV, and film use his house for their programs. That's pretty cool considering he was homeless. His story is similar to mine in some ways. God can do the impossible through someone's life.

You would never know my brotha Vince owns a house like this, because he and his wife are very humble. As a matter of fact, I am the one who brags on what God has done in and through his life.

When I got back to El Paso, we started visiting each other's areas, but we both were thinking the same thing. We both knew we did some pretty cool things in God's kingdom. We were both thinking, *"How much of an offering we should give?"* So I said, "Look, let me bring you out first and I'll take care of you and then I'll go out with you." Next thing you know Vince was on a flight to El Paso.

When he arrived, we picked him up at the airport and took him to his hotel. I walked into his hotel room with him and asked him if the room was satisfactory? He said 'Yes'. We always leave a basket with snacks and drinks for our guests to have something to munch on.

I told him what time to be ready because I was taking him out to eat. We take our guest speakers out to lunch and dinner, sometimes breakfast, too, plus they get a good offering. I remember Vince saying, "You do things on a whole other level. Whoever taught you taught you well."

This is true. I learn all this from Pastor Krishna when he comes out with us. He taught me to treat guest speakers with excellence. Sometimes people get mad when I say this, but I could care less. I'm building God's kingdom. The way I look at it is that if drug dealers, movie stars, and porn stars are blessed at this level when they blaspheme my God and live for the worlds system, then there shouldn't be a problem if men and women of God get blessed. I'm here to love God and love people for God's glory. Nothing is going to detour me from that.

I took Vince to many places to preach. He had a great time. I introduced him to a few of the pastors I ordained into my ministry. I also took him to Juarez, Mexico. He loved it, and he was fearless for God just like I was. I prayed and thanked God for connecting me to straight up soldiers in his kingdom.

After Vince went back to California, it was my turn to go out to his area and preach the gospel. God answered my prayers about opening doors for me all over California. Little did I know the people I would meet and how much I would be preaching in California.

I arrived in LA to preach with Vince, and he got me this amazing hotel, much nicer than anything I could have ever put him in El Paso. He walked me to my room like I did for him in El Paso.

"Is this room satisfactory to you?"

I laughed, "It sure is."

He said, "I'll be here at so and so time to take you to eat. You know how we do it."

We both laughed. One thing I can say is I've always tried to connect as many preachers I could so they could expand their reach in the kingdom of God. It doesn't matter if you do ministry at a bigger or smaller level than me, if I can help anyone do bigger things in God's kingdom and make a dent in the devil's territory, than I'm all for it. I'm not jealous and understand we need to stand united as a unit and impact this world for God's glory.

If you are my brother or sister in Christ, we are on the same side. We should stand together.

Vince actually told me, "It's been really rare when I've met someone like you with so many connections in God's kingdom, and you're younger than me, which really trips me out."

I was honored by his words. We have a mutual respect for each other, and our wives hit it off. They got along great.

Now it was my turn to go to hit the streets with him in LA. It was my birthday. We were getting clothes, food and drinks ready to take to the streets of skid row in LA. Vince has a big trailer he takes with him when he goes to feed the hungry and clothe the poor. We were going to preach to gangsters and homeless people, my favorite people to preach to. I look upon it as the best birthday I've ever had. Vince showed me around and I couldn't believe what I was seeing.

Block after block, neighborhood after neighborhood, it must have been miles of non-stop tents and sleeping bags with homeless people, gang members, and prostitutes everywhere. It really tripped me out. That's when I realized the devil has legion spirits and strongholds of different kinds in different cities everywhere. It dawned on me how important it was that believers in Christ need to be lights in this dark world for God's glory. This world needs hope.

That day Evelyn and our four kids were with us doing ministry on the skid row streets. It was amazing. Guys came up to us getting clothes, food, and drinks from us, also prayer and the testimony of Jesus. Almost everyone I talked to knew I came from the streets too, so it was really easy to minister to them because I could relate to them. Many accepted Jesus that day as their Lord and Savior.

After this I preached at the men's ministry at 7:00 a.m. on a Saturday morning. Again the service was awesome. Then I preached for Vince's pastor. It was awesome. Their building was like a theater where Broadway shows were performed. They took me to eat after service, and we had an amazing conversation. They had done such amazing things in God's kingdom with many of the greats that had passed away and were now in heaven. They had been on worldwide TV, written books, and traveled the world on a private jet. Their stories were amazing and inspiring.

I told them about Pastor Krishna and everyone I'd met preaching, and they told me about their mentor and pastor. He was a really well known preacher that had died in a plane crash. I sympathized with them over the loss of their mentor. I told them it would be hard for me without Pastor Krishna around. They told Evelyn and me that it had been an honor meeting us and that we were an amazing couple. They thought that we reminded them of themselves when they were younger. Evelyn and I felt the honor was ours, and told them so. We considered them generals in God's kingdom. It was an amazing experience. We've since preached for them multiple times. They even gave us an amazing letter thanking us for always preaching for them, and how much of an impact we had on their church. It really touched me and my wife. They are much older than us, but I still plan on hooking them up to preach in our area one of these days. It is a blessing knowing them.

50.

New Friends

I was preaching all over the place by this time, and going to many conferences. My favorite conference to go to is at ALFC in El Paso, partly because Pastor Krishna goes, but also because I love everyone there. This is where I met a great friend of mine out of Fort Stockton, Texas named Victor Lopez. He pastors a great church out there. Eventually he invited me to preach at his church.

Conferences usually provide a place for preachers to sit down and eat together so you can mingle. This is how I met him. I'm a big jokester and I'm usually one of the loudest ones, always having a good time joking around, which is not always normal. Many preachers act all serious and proper. I'm not out of line but I enjoy having a good time in Christ.

Victor was sitting across the table from me and I noticed he had a tattoo on his forearm. I asked him really loudly, "Is that a tattoo on your arm?"

He said, "Yes."

"What does it stand for?" Before he could answer, I said, "It's the street gang you represent."

A lot of ministers looked at our table and started cracking up. I was laughing at him too. I messed with him, joking around with him for quite a while. I explained to him how I used to live crazy. I said, "Don't worry. I got prison style tattoos myself."

Pastor Krishna was sitting next to me telling him, "He's not lying."

So the next day, our special seating for preachers had labeled stickers on the seats with your name on it. As I sat down, I saw my brother Victor getting directions to his seating. Wouldn't you know it? His seat was right next to mine. I had a big smile on my face because of the night before. I was going to joke around with him again. As he got closer to me, I didn't even get the chance. He started yelling, "Am I sitting here next to this guy? I don't want to sit next to him." Then he started laughing at me, saying, "I'm a jokester too. You ain't the only one." We hugged each other and started laughing.

I knew we would be doing things together for God's glory after Victor got to know me and knew my life story. I messed and joked around with him quite a bit until he got tired of it and started messing around with me too. He told me after we got to know each other, that he didn't know how much he could joke around with me because of my past. That made me laugh.

He said, "I'm serious bro, you were a hardcore street dude. But after you would joke around so much with me, I got tired of it and started messing with you back." It's always a pleasure to see my brotha Victor and his wife Valerie. They are really good people.

The reason I bring up my brotha Victor in my story is because he's the one that kept telling me, "You need to write a book, bro. I believe it will be really big and I believe a movie will come out of it too."

I'd laugh when he'd say this, but truth be told, I had already been approached a few times about a book. I really didn't want to, to be honest. I wanted people's eyes on Jesus, not me.

Victor would say, "It's about Jesus, bro, you have the most intense testimony of anyone I know. You've got to do it." He'd tell me this when we saw each other over the years.

Gina had told me this many years ago when she got me saved. When I was locked up she would say, "Huero, you're gonna have a book out one day, and a movie too, glorifying God."

It just seemed so far-fetched. I couldn't believe it. I thought back then, *"Yeah, right, I'm locked down in this cell and I'm gonna write a book"* It just didn't seem realistic or possible, but at the time I didn't know my God was the God of the impossible like I do now.

Around this time I was headed back out to preach at many churches from Southern to Northern California, my west coast preaching tour, as I call it.

When I got to LA, I hooked up with my brotha Vince. I was on my way to preach at the men's ministry again. I preached a sermon titled *Pressure: What's In You?* I was being my normal self: talking about dreaming big for God and just being real. All the guys loved it. Afterward, everyone was coming up to me thanking me for coming which is a usual occurrence. They took me to a side room in the church facility to meet some people who had come to see me preach. There were around seven guys in the room.

They introduced me to Sal Rodriguez and Blinky Rodriguez. I asked them how they liked the sermon. They told me it was awesome and they really liked it.

"Great, it's nice to meet you guys." Then the person introducing us said, "Isaiah, Sal Rodriguez is of the music band WAR. They used to sing Low Rider, Cisco Kid, and Why Can't We Be Friends?"

I stopped him and said, "Yeah, I know the group WAR, who doesn't?" I turned to Sal. "You're the drummer of the mega band WAR. I have your greatest hits CD in my car right now. I still listen to you guys until this very day. How long have you been serving God?"

He told me, and then I said, "You know what really touches me about meeting you? It's not that you're famous. What touches my heart about you is that you love God. It *is* pretty cool you're in the WAR band." It tripped me out that he had come to hear me preach.

I also met Blinky Rodriguez who was a really famous martial artist. Blinky was a really cool guy. You could tell he was a fighter because of his intensity level. We were talking about Jesus and he was getting really excited. He made a fist with one of his hands and started punching his other open hand so hard when talking about Jesus that his watch broke off his wrist and fell on the floor. He made me laugh so hard my stomach hurt.

I said, "Hey carnal Blinky, you're trying to beat Jesus into someone right now." I started telling everyone in the room, "Hey, Blinky's trying to beat Jesus into someone right now." Everyone laughed.

I met another guy in the room who said to me, "Man, I really loved your preaching. You're fearless when it comes to preaching the gospel. I haven't seen that type of boldness and preaching since the 80's"

I also met the pastor I was preaching for the next day. I really liked everyone I met. We all had fun talking and walking outside together. Sal and Blinky started giving me the history about San Fernando, California. They explained how so much talent came from that city and they named many famous people everyone reading this book would know about. They pointed out the high school, which was across the street, and said everyone we mentioned went to that high school. "We did too."

They liked me so much that they started talking to one another and said, "Hey, let's take Pastor Isaiah to go eat." They told me all the famous people they mentioned go to this
Mexican restaurant.

When we got there they got us a table in a side room where we fit comfortably and could talk. I sat right across from Blinky, and my brotha Vince sat right next to me. Sal sat maybe four seats away from me. Blinky was still trying to fix his watch. The little pin that held the watch together had popped out when it fell.

"Let me fix that for you, Blinky." I put the pin back in the part that held the watch together fairly quickly. He thanked me.

We all ordered. I believe I ordered menudo.

Blinky and I really hit it off. Vince told me everyone was laughing when Blinky and I were talking to each other. He said it was funny because everyone could tell Blinky and I both had strong personalities. We were talking about God non-stop. They said we both were so excited we were cutting each other off mid- sentence because we were both so excited talking about Jesus.

Blinky said, "You're here with us because you obviously do things at another level or you wouldn't be sitting here with us, am I right?"

I said, "You're right."

"Who do we talk to when we deal with stuff? We can't talk to just anyone."

I said, "You're 100 percent right."

Blinky told me things he had dealt with when life got hard, and I did the same, but one thing he dealt with really exemplified his love and faith towards God. It really touched my heart.  His son had been killed by gang violence. He told me to read up on it, that everything had been documented and was in public records. Blinky explained how people loved him and wanted revenge. I knew he wasn't lying because at the men's meeting you could see immediately how much everyone respected him. Instead of getting revenge, he did the unthinkable. He forgave the individuals and made peace with them. He showed them the love of Christ. It was very powerful and profound. He loved them and sought a peaceful resolution. I was amazed. It showed his character. I'm not saying anyone is perfect, but wow, this was such a testament to God's love and forgiveness.

I admitted to Blinky I didn't know if I could do the same thing he did. It really blew my mind. I consider Blinky an awesome man of God. Anyone that can't get some type of inspiration out of talking to someone like Blinky Rodriguez is just playing ignorant; at least that's how I feel.

We talked about many other things. Blinky also does many great things for his community and has helped keep gang violence down. It really was my honor to meet Blinky from the San Fernando Valley in California. We exchanged numbers and keep in contact with each other.

While Blinky and I were talking I would yell out to Sal, "Hey my brotha Sal, what do you do when you're on tour? Do you say Jesus loves you? Now here's some Slippin into Darkness for you," which is a big hit by the band WAR. I would start laughing.

He would look at me and say, "No, Pastor Isaiah, Why Can't We Be Friends?" which is another really big hit by WAR, which you may have heard on movies or movie soundtracks. We both laughed. I think he liked me joking around with him, which I did throughout our lunch because it probably made him feel normal being around me, messing around and joking with him. I'm pretty sure if people knew who he was they would be in awe and not treat him like a normal human being. I was used to being around really big name preachers who I'd been honored to meet or eat with at conferences, and I always treated them normal. I recognized their amazing talents and gifts, but still to me they are not Jesus Christ, the real and only superstar that makes it possible for us to have an eternal home in heaven.

Another thing I've noticed about being around really successful people is when you meet them they are really down to earth. They are just like you and me. They just choose to dream while awake with their eyes wide open as I do.

After the meal, my brotha Sal asked where I was preaching the next day. I told him and he said, "I know the place. I'll be there and I said, "Cool, that would be awesome." We exchanged phone numbers and as we walked out, Blinky, Vince and I still talked for a while.

Blinky said, "I need to give you something before you leave." He looked in his pants pockets and pulled out his personal anointing oil he used to pray for people and gave it to me. It was an experience I will never forget. Vince took me back to my hotel where Evelyn was waiting for me. I told her, "You'll never believe who came to see me preach today." I told her about everyone.

"Sal Rodriguez from WAR came to see me, and then we all went to eat."

"Oh, Isaiah, you weren't messing with him, were you?"

"You know me. I sure was."

"Oh, he will probably never want to see you again."

"Actually, he loved it. He's coming to see us tomorrow."

She couldn't believe it. "Boy, I cannot believe the favor God has put on your life. Instead of people getting offended with you, they love you."

I laughed. The next morning I was off to preach at a church I'd never been to. I saw my brotha Sal come into the church and sit down to hear me preach.

After service, my wife and I prayed for people. Many were touched by the Holy Spirit. After we finished praying, I talked to people as usual. Everyone bought CDs, DVDs, and magazines with my testimony and photos of me from my past. These purchases fund my ministry.

It always trips me out. Everywhere I preached people wanted me to sign my CDs or magazines. They would ask me, "Could you sign your merchandise for me?" I would say, "I'm not famous, only Jesus Christ is, but sure, if you would like me to sign what you're buying from me, I can do that for you." I always put a saying under my signature like *Dream Big* or *God's Great.*

After I finished, me and my brotha Sal started talking. I told him signing my signature on people's stuff kinda tripped me out.

"It comes with the territory, my brotha."

Since we were talking about signatures I said, "Hey bro, let me go get my WAR's greatest hits CD so you could sign it for me."

He said, "Isaiah, you're like a modern day apostle Paul."

I laughed.

Then he said, "I know the pastor is going to take you guys to eat in a little bit, so I'm gonna call you and take you some stuff God told me to give to you. No need for a signature on your CD."

I said, "OK."

"I'm on my way to the studio. I shouldn't be there long, and then I'll get the address of the restaurant you're at and take you your stuff, OK?"

I said, "Alright."

The pastor took me to eat. There were around ten of us eating, talking, and having a good time. Sal called and I gave him the address where we were eating. He showed up. What he was about to do was gonna touch my heart and bring my wife to tears.

He had a bag full of stuff for me. It was WAR memorabilia. Everything had been signed by my brotha Sal. There were signed and painted drum sticks that also had some of their songs written on them like Lowrider and Cisco Kid. There was also a signed greatest hits CD by WAR, a signed a photograph of WAR, also a drum cover with Sal's face painted on it, which is a popular logo they use.

The drum cover said *Why Can't We Be Friends* in big letters written by Sal himself. That was one of their biggest hits. Everything he gave me was written out to me personally. Now Sal didn't know, but God did stuff like this that touched my heart. I considered things given to me like that very special. I have a collection of things; either given to me or signed by great men of God, that always give me good memories and remind me how far my sweet Jesus has brought me in life. I'm not perfect but I am so far from the person I once was before meeting my King.

My brotha Sal also gave me multiple CDs of artists he either produced or worked with; some famous and some up and comers who used their platforms for Jesus Christ. The CDs touched me so much when I listened to them. I can't get enough of them. They are amazing artists who make Godly oldies or Godly Rap records. They are very inspiring and unique to say the least.

My wife Beautiful was crying, thanking my brotha Sal and hugging him. I was very touched as well. We got some photos with him holding up everything he had given us. He said God told him to do that for us. It is definitely a memory engrafted in my mind and heart. I will never forget when Sal left. I remember the pastors and everyone there that knew him saying, "Man, you must have some type of favor on your life. We've known him for years and he's never given us anything like that." It was really cool.

Sal and I keep in contact, talking every few days or texting each other. God's a Great God and worthy to be praised. I got back to El Paso feeling blessed and showing off the amazing CDs and songs Sal gave me which everyone loved. The gifts really blew my mind and are a weapon of warfare unto our enemy.

I had to go back to the LA area for my little sister's wedding. Sal had called me around three days before I was going out to LA. He was on tour but would be there when I got there. He asked if I was preaching. I asked why, and he said, "So I could check you out."

"No, I'm going for a wedding. I'll be in LA around five days."

"Why don't you let me work my magic and hook you up to preach out here?"

I said, "Cool, sounds great."

My wife booked a hotel in the exact city Sal lives in. He called me and asked, "Where you at?"

When I told him he said, "Bro, you're right down the street from my house."

"Wow, well God knows what he's doing, huh?"

Sal said, "I'm gonna text you my address so you could pick me up and so you can see the studios in my house."

He'd actually coordinated for me to preach later that night. So since Sal had hooked me up with signed memorabilia it was my turn to hook him up. I had a cross with diamonds in it I was giving him from my personal jewelry. I also gave him some CDs of my preaching along with a magazine I was in. I signed it for him too. We also brought him different flavored pistachios. He loved the pistachios and started eating them immediately.

He showed us his home studios were the hits go down. It was cool.

"Do you mind if I ride with you guys where I've hooked you up to preach?"

I said, "Of course not." So off we went.

Sal surprised me with a new CD. He put it on while we were driving and man it was awesome. They were amazing godly songs. I remember Sal telling me on one of the songs he was playing how he heard this certain artist growing up at concerts and how he now records music with him. He said, "It blows my mind." As he said this he was tapping on my dashboard in the car, singing.

I thought to myself I can totally understand that. I never thought in my wildest dreams I would be rolling in California with the drummer of the mega band WAR sitting in my car taking me to preach somewhere. It blew my mind too.

Sal asked if we'd eaten. We told him no.

"Turn here, there's a great place to eat here. I'm gonna take you there."

When we got there and we were ordering, I remember laughing and telling the girl waiting us, "You don't know who this is, do you?" I looked at Sal and said, "People don't know who you are, do they?"

I said to the waiter, "This is Sal Rodriguez, you know, from the mega band WAR."

She said, "I'm younger."

"It don't matter. Their songs come out on movies shows all around the world." I sang her a few including Why Can't We Be Friends. She knew immediately who he was then. She said, "Wow!"

Sal said, "This man here is a famous evangelist preacher. This is Isaiah Blancas."

She said, "You guys made my day."

The food was great, and a man came up to our table and said to me, "You love God, don't you?"

I said, "Yes, I do," which was quite normal for me. It happened quite a bit. You could tell Sal tripped out a little. I prayed and preached to this guy. Sal also talked to him. It was a blessing.

We got back on our way to the preaching engagement. When we got there, I saw we were at a house, not a church. When we walked into the house I saw big old camera lights, couches, and posters and things hanging on the wall.

Sal had told me to dress normal, not in my preacher clothes. I now understood why. I was coming out on a show with famous comedian, Gilbert Esquivel. Sal introduced us and we said 'Hi'.

I told him "I've got a great sermon."

Gilbert said, "You're not preaching a sermon."

"What?"

"You're coming out on my show. Put your Bible away. You'll see. Just go with the flow. We're going live in a few minutes."

It really tripped me out. Sal looked at my face because I looked puzzled. Gilbert told me and Sal to sit on the couch together so we could be introduced by him and his sidekick named Lulu, who was a singer. I was getting ready for the show to start, not really knowing what I was supposed to do. My wife Evelyn was behind the scenes. God was getting me ready for something new and exciting.

So the show started. There were many viewers. You could tell by the TV screens that we could see. People were literally tuning in from around the country and many places around the world. You can tune in through social media on Gilbert's show. Comments and likes were popping up on the screens non-stop throughout the show.

Gilbert first introduced Sal. Gilbert, Lulu, and Sal were talking to the viewers. Then Gilbert said, "We have a special guest with us tonight. Please welcome Isaiah Blancas from El Paso, Texas."

Gilbert asked me, "So you're a preacher, huh?"

"Yeah."

"I would've never known, because you look like a mean creature." He was doing his comedy thing. I remember seeing the big TV screens with comments saying, "Mean creature," with smiley and laughing emojis. It was funny.

Now on Gilbert's show, they talk to the viewers, and then play different type of songs. As Gilbert did his comedy act, which was really funny, I was having a great time, but I was thinking, *"OK, when do I preach or talk about God?"* I was about to find out how everything worked as the two-hour show kept rolling along. I was enjoying myself.

Gilbert said, "Let's play a WAR song for all the viewers." The song was *Don't Let No One Get You Down,* which is an all-time favorite. Sal pulled out some bongos he had brought and started playing the bongos and singing to the song. It really tripped me out. I had been around many big named preachers but never people who did big things in the entertainment world. It was something totally new, fresh and exciting for me.

I kinda saw where God was going with this. I was sitting there hearing a song I've always loved. It really hit me. I'm sitting here on a show with a famous comedian, an amazing singer Lulu, and Sal, the drummer of WAR who rolled with me here, and I was a special guest. I was thankful to God for his favor and grace upon my life. It was pretty cool, but to all reading this book: I had believed the unbelievable and had always had great expectations. To me, in God, nothing was impossible.

Gilbert started interviewing me more and asking more questions about my past lifestyle, and everyone on that show was tripping out on my testimony. Comments by viewers showed my testimony was touching them too. It was great. They started playing Godly oldies and rap for me and I loved it.

Gilbert tripped out because my wife and I would go to prisons and some of the worst ghettos in Juarez, Mexico.

He said, "Wow, you and your wife go out there to preach yet they tell everyone in America not to go into Juarez because it's very dangerous and that they have lookouts out there just waiting to harm and rob you."

I laughed. Beautiful was yelling behind the scenes, "Don't go in a nice car, walk across!" She kept yelling things out so Gilbert said, "Brother, why don't you introduce your wife to the viewers?"

Her eyes practically popped out. She's not the type to want to be in the public eye. Gilbert would not accept no for an answer so Evelyn was even on the show.

Gilbert was so touched by my testimony that he invited me to preach the next day at one of his shows he was performing. When the show was about to end Gilbert said, "Isaiah, why don't you preach to the people watching for a while. Preach whatever you feel God has placed in your heart for our viewers."

So I did, and it was God flowing through this willing vessel, touching people's minds, hearts, and souls. After I preached for a while, they played one last song before the show ended. Everyone but me was dancing around like crazy people, but it was amazing because they were crazy for Jesus Christ. You could feel the Holy Spirit big time. It was such a great time.

After the show ended, we all talked for a good while. Gilbert gave us souvenirs. He gives gifts to all guests who come out on the show. We exchanged phone numbers on the spot and talk every few days or text each other.

When we were leaving, Gilbert told Evelyn and me, "You're family now. Whenever you both are in Southern California, you stay at my house with me. I have extra bedrooms."

It really touched my heart. I offered the same thing back to Gilbert. "If you're ever in the El Paso area, you stay with us too."

It was such a great experience and I know it's not my last. Gilbert, Sal and I have already coordinated dates to do ministry for God together. God was opening doors for Sal and Gilbert through me to get into more of a ministry environment where they could get connected with more pastors and churches. Also, God was opening doors through Sal and Gilbert for me to be able to cross over and preach in the entertainment world. It was so clear now to me what God was doing.

I've told Gilbert that his show is such a unique way to preach to the secular world and reel them in for God to touch them. What Gilbert does is not so different from what I do. He gets on their level to relate to his viewers, and then hits them right between their eyes with the gospel of Jesus Christ. It's awesome. It's like when I preach to hard core gangsters. I get on their level to relate to them, and then I do the same. I can honestly say that my God, my sweet Jesus has been so good to me through ups and downs, highs and lows. My sweet Jesus has always been with me, helping me and guiding me through the good and the bad this life brings in.

Epilogue: Just the Beginning

The story you've just read shows you my highs and my lows, but one thing I can say for sure is - even when times are hard and you feel as if there's no hope, remember the most
important thing I've ever done in my life is accepting Jesus Christ as my Lord and Savior. I don't know what my future holds but my God does, and I can say without a shadow of doubt that my God is a great God.

If you've never accepted Jesus Christ as your Lord and Savior, you need to do so right now. You are not reading this book by accident. You are precious to Jesus just as you are. It doesn't matter how bad you think you are; you are never too far gone for God's amazing grace and love to rescue you from your sins. He sent his Son Jesus to die for your sins so you can truly be free. Your mess can become a masterpiece, and your tests can be come testimonies.

I want to lead you into a quick prayer a prayer of salvation. It doesn't matter where you are. You can be in a cell locked up as I was. You can be sick in a hospital. You can feel so undeserving, as if you can never be forgiven.

Let me remind you - even the great stories in the Bible were men and women who were imperfect but knew they needed a perfect loving Father.

Pray this prayer with me: "Jesus, I know I'm a sinner. I know I've fallen short, but I also know you died for my sins. I repent Jesus, and ask you to wash my sins with your precious blood. I accept you now as my Lord and Savior. Amen."

If you've prayed this prayer you are now saved! Find yourself a good local church and grow in God. I thank God for you and I believe you will revolutionize this earth with God's Word. Be radical for Jesus and save as many souls as you possibly can.

Your brother in Christ Jesus,
Evangelist Isaiah Blancas
Dream Big!

Email Isaiah at IsaiahVRC@gmail.com

Email Jody Bailey Day at jodybooks@faithwriters.net

Made in the USA
Columbia, SC
07 March 2021

33633486R00133